THE ARCHITECTURAL PLANNING OF
ST. PETERSBURG

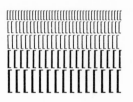

The Architectural Planning of St. Petersburg

By Iurii Alekseevich Egorov

Translated by Eric Dluhosch

OHIO UNIVERSITY PRESS

Athens, Ohio   1969

Preface

It was Colin Rowe, Chairman of the Department of Urban Planning at Cornell University, who first introduced me to the Russian edition of this book. Like him, I was intrigued by some of the plan diagrams which, in turn, directed my interest to the text.

In our time the art of planning has achieved a high degree of sophistication. Yet many of our cities are chaotic, ugly, and undeniably unpleasant to live in. Though the works of Camillo Sitte, Kevin Lynch, and architects such as Saarinen are being discussed among architects and planners, architectural history has tended to concern itself with single buildings rather than complete environments. The development of St. Petersburg is remarkable precisely because it was based on an understanding of the complete environment.

In tracing the planning of this city, Egorov has illuminated aspects of urban design that transcend the particular. He has shown how each of the 18th and 19th century planners tried to relate his contribution to the already existing spaces of the city and took care to work within the limitations established by the natural site, historical precedent, climatic conditions, and social and political changes. In its broader context this presupposes a marriage of the arts and the integration of individual parts into an organic whole. It requires a subordination of the minor to the major theme, and the subordination of the star performer—eager to create a masterpiece—to the demands of the overall plan. I believe that by showing how St. Petersburg achieved both character and beauty Egorov has pointed a lesson of relevance to the urban designers of today.

The translator wishes to acknowledge his gratitude to Mrs. Fannia Weingartner for her expert advice and patience in transforming the following translation into a fully comprehensible manuscript.

ERIC DLUHOSCH

Contents

List of Maps, Charts, and Illustrations

Translator's note on the founding and development of St. Petersburg

The history of St. Petersburg—now called Leningrad—is inextricably bound up with the emergence of Russia as a major European power and its transformation from a medieval Byzantine empire into a modern global superpower. Looking back to the century preceding the French Revolution, one finds that four European rulers stand out among all the others as the most powerful representatives of enlightened despotism during this period: Louis XIV, Frederick the Great, Peter the Great, and Catherine the Great. It is interesting to note that two of these were sovereigns of Russia.[1] Both Peter the Great and Catherine the Great set out to make Russia a powerful equal of the family of nations and both spared no effort to increase her influence in international affairs while at the same time transforming Russia into a modern state on the model of the other European countries. But it is Peter the Great who must be credited with providing the initial impetus that revolutionized the ancient kingdom of Muscovy and, over the opposition of his reluctant subjects, opened the door to Western influence in all areas of national life. The founding of St. Petersburg as the new capital of the Russian Empire in 1703 is a concrete symbol of this great transformation.

While relentlessly pursuing a policy of reform at home, Peter directed his policy toward establishing Russia as an equal partner among the other nations of Europe. One of the most persistent aspects of this policy was his desire to provide Russia with adequate maritime outlets, especially toward the West. The traditional port connecting Russia with the other maritime powers had up to now been the port of Arkhangelsk, which due to its remoteness and its inaccessibility during the winter had its obvious disadvantages.[2] Azov, the port on the Sea of Azov, was conquered by Peter in 1696, but had to be surrendered to the Turks in 1713. In the meantime Peter had made several attempts to find suitable harbor sites in the North —such as Rogervik near Reval—which had proved unsuccessful.[3] All the other territory suitable for harbor building was at that time controlled by the Swedes. Thus the Great Northern War between Russia and Sweden, lasting from 1700 to 1721, was begun by Peter to gain access to the Baltic Sea.

In order to understand the full background of Peter I's efforts to gain a foothold in the Baltic it is necessary to take a brief glance at the history of this territory.

Long before Peter I established himself in the delta of the Neva River, the site of the future city of St. Petersburg had

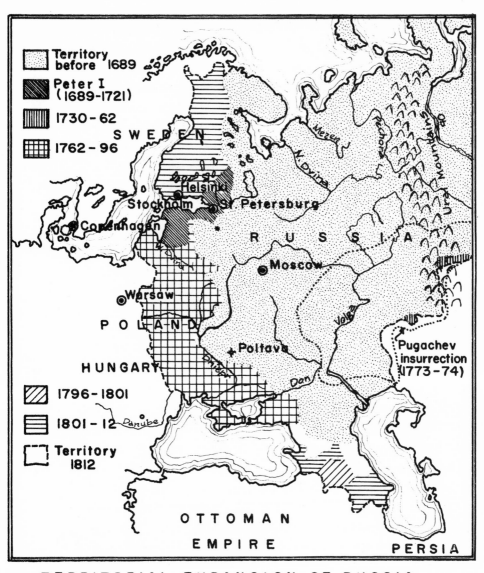

Legend:
- Territory before 1689
- Peter I (1689-1721)
- 1730-62
- 1762-96
- 1796-1801
- 1801-12
- Territory 1812

Labels on map:

SWEDEN

Helsinki
Stockholm — St. Petersburg
Copenhagen

RUSSIA

Moscow

Warsaw

POLAND

Poltava

HUNGARY

Danube

Dnieper

Don

Volga

Mezen

N. Dvina

Pechora

Ural Mountains

Pugachev insurrection (1773-74)

OTTOMAN EMPIRE

PERSIA

TERRITORIAL EXPANSION OF RUSSIA
1689 — 1812

become a thriving colony of Novgorod merchants. Novgorod had already grown into an important trading center in the earliest times. It became the connecting center between Scandinavia and northern Russia with the great water road going south through Kiev to the Black Sea. Indeed, even before the founding of the independent state of Novgorod, the Roos and the Gothland Vikings had long used this trade route from Varjag in Sweden down the Neva into Lake Ladoga and on to Holmgard (later Novgorod). In time the connection between the Varjagians on the eastern shores of the Baltic and their kindred in the West was severed and Novgorod developed into a powerful state with territories extending from Lake Ilmen to the White Sea and eastward to the Ural Mountains. Its possessions included the southern shore of the Gulf of Finland, including the site of what was to become St. Petersburg.

In the 10th century the shippers of Novgorod, mostly Norsemen, in concert with the Gothlanders and later with the Hanseatic merchants carried on a lively trade with the rest of Europe. It was by the Volga-Ilmen-Neva route that the wares of Central Asia reached England long before the Norman Conquest.

The power and prosperity of Novgorod did not remain unthreatened. In 1240, during the reign of Grand Duke Alexander, a force led by the Swedish general, Berger Jarl, prepared to attack Novgorod in the name of a crusade against the Eastern Orthodox heretics ordered by the Pope on behalf of the Roman Catholic Church. The Grand Duke Alexander defeated the Swedes in a battle on the Neva River, later taking the name Nevski in memory of this feat. He became a legendary figure and one of the earliest national heroes of Russia and was later canonized by the Russian Orthodox Church. Sixty years later the Swedes returned and eventually established a firm foothold on the left bank of the Neva. Here they built the fortress of Landskrona in an effort to maintain their conquest. Before long, however, the Novgorodians destroyed the fortress and drove the Swedes away.

Later, in the 16th century, Ivan the Terrible attempted to conquer the Baltic by gaining access to the West through Livonia. The war began in 1558 and lasted for twenty-four years. At first he met with great success, but later the concerted efforts of Poland-Lithuania, Sweden, and Denmark forced Ivan to relinquish all his previous gains.[4] The Swedes built another fort higher upstream at Okhta which came to be known as Ny-skantze or Nienschanz. A flourishing town developed around the fortress. In the latter part of the century it became so prosperous that it boasted a fleet of a few hundred ships. To defend the source of the river the Swedes built yet another fort, Noteburg, which the Novgorodians called Oreshka. (Peter I later gave it the name Schlüsselberg, indulging his predilection for Dutch and German names—one not at all shared by his xenophobic Muscovite subjects who in general tended to despise anything foreign and in particular anything German.)

It was Peter I who finally ended Swedish claims to this region and who succeeded in permanently annexing this hard-fought-for territory to the rest of the Russian Empire. By the time the war came to an end the Swedes were totally exhausted and barely able to maintain themselves as a second class power. Peter, flushed with success in gaining access to the Baltic, decided to demonstrate Russia's intention to hold on to this territory forever by founding the city of St. Petersburg on the banks of the Neva. This was to be his "paradise" and "window looking into Europe."

Another important influence on the development of St. Petersburg was Peter's effort to put into practice the lessons

House of Romanov

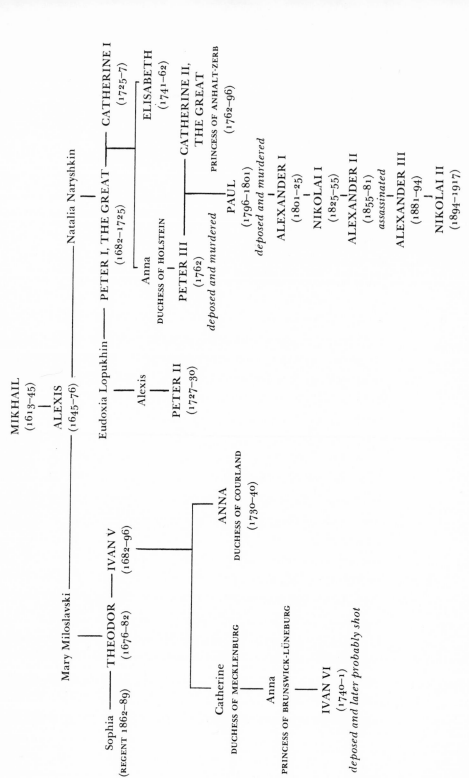

he had learned while visiting Holland and England during his trip abroad as a member of the so-called "great embassy." As early as 1697 large groups of Russians had been sent abroad to receive military training and to learn the arts of navigation. The "great embassy" was a natural sequel to this policy. In charge of the group was "min Heer Peter Mikhailov" who was nobody else but Peter I himself, officially incognito—a ruse that fooled nobody.[5] Peter and his train spent their time abroad absorbing Western customs and techniques. While working in the shipyards of Amsterdam and during his subsequent travels in the rest of Europe, Peter recruited a number of foreigners to return to Russia with him, mostly skilled craftsmen and shipbuilders, as well as other specialists and military and naval experts. He observed and was impressed by Dutch planning efficiency, a lesson which was later applied to the planning of St. Petersburg. According to Peter's own words that city was to be laid out "in the manner of the Dutch" with regular blocks and straight canals penetrating the territory of the city at right angles to each other.

In addition to his admiration for the Dutch Peter was motivated by his desire to distinguish the new capital from the traditional Russian city, particularly Moscow, which symbolized so much of what he wanted to reform.[6] He had in mind a well-ordered city with straight streets lined with densely packed brick buildings with high, tiled roofs and with a multitude of turrets and towers strikingly scattered about the city. All of this was in direct contrast to the traditional Russian way of city building. Usually a house was placed in the center of a lot with its service facilities—kitchens, storage areas, and stables—clustered at the periphery fronting the street. While the central core of these complexes was often very picturesque, the street itself was forced into narrow, crooked, and tortuous shapes according to the individual

owner's whim in the construction of the estate's service facilities.[7] To halt this encroachment of the service facilities onto
the streets, Peter decreed the implementation of the so-called
"red line." This line was staked out on each site establishing
uniform limits beyond which no building was allowed to pro-
trude.[8] Moreover, a definite set of designs, which everyone
was obliged to follow, was imposed upon the population
predicated on status and means.[9]

A study of Peter's numerous and often seemingly contra-
dictory ukases reveals that he was preoccupied with a consistent set of prerequisites which formed the basis for the early
planning of St. Petersburg.[10] These were to:

1. Create a well-built, modern city with all conveniences,
   with straight streets lined with dense brick houses, and
   large gardens.
2. Incorporate waterways such as the Neva, the canals, and
   the channels into the general plan.
3. Require that all buildings conform to strict specifications.
4. Settle each strata of population into a particular section
   of the city.
5. Organize the commercial and industrial communities in
   order to concentrate the management of the city in their
   hands.[11]

Unfortunately, Peter's enthusiasm for his new capital was
shared neither by his Muscovite subjects nor by the Church
which regarded this region as the gate to Hades if not hell
itself. But opposition proved of no avail against the iron will
of the Tsar. Though the priests called him Antichrist and the
Church excommunicated him, Peter persisted in his plan. His
opponents were thrown into dungeons or executed. When his
own son, Alexis, became the tool of the opposition, Peter did
not hesitate and sacrificed him as well.

On May 7, 1703, at the helm of their newly built flotilla
of thirty ships, Peter I and his lifelong friend Prince Alex-

ander Menshikov, sailed down the Neva and captured the Swedish fortress Nienschanz, located on the north side of the river. On May 16, Peter established himself in the fortress, and this date has been accepted as the founding day of St. Petersburg. On June 29, the fortress was named by Peter "Sankt Pieter Burkh" in honor of St. Peter. Later, when a church commemorating St. Peter and St. Paul was built within the fortress, it became known as the Peter and Paul Fortress and the name Sankt Pieter Burkh was relegated to the community growing up around the fortress.[12]

The construction of the city commenced with the building of the Peter and Paul Fortress, a project which employed twenty thousand men. As the fortress rose amidst the marshes so did the city itself. Peter built himself a small house nearby and personally supervised the progress of the building. The conditions under which the laborers had to exist during the early years of St. Petersburg's construction were terrible beyond belief. The climate was unhealthy, while the water was unfit for drinking. The territory was periodically threatened by great floods, such as that of 1705, which inundated Peter's camp and undermined the walls of the newly constructed fortifications. The Swedish prisoners of war and the thousands of conscripted laborers were so ravaged by dysentery and physical exhaustion that by 1710 Peter had to find additional labor. In that year he issued an ukase ordering the governments of the interior to furnish forty thousand laborers together with their most essential tools. These people cut through the growth, drained the swamps, dredged the river, dug canals, raised earthen dams and embankments, drove piles into the soft ground, and gradually accomplished the building of St. Petersburg.[13] Within three years the new city devoured an army of one hundred and fifty thousand workers.

But Peter showed no mercy; on the contrary, he merely took stronger action.

On October 9, 1714 he issued an ukase prohibiting masonry construction throughout all of Russia:

> Masonry construction is advancing slowly because of the difficulties in finding stonemasons and other related craftsmen. Therefore it is forbidden in the whole empire to build any masonry structure whatever upon the penalty of exile and banishment.[14]

Another ukase in the same month regulated the procurement of materials:

> All vessels entering St. Petersburg via Lake Ladoga and also all vehicles and transport arriving in the city by land routes carrying other merchandise, must bring along as well a load of stones.[15]

Imperial decrees were necessary not only to build the new capital but also to populate it. Given the climate, living conditions, and the general atmosphere prevailing in the city at that time, nobody was particularly eager to settle there voluntarily. So Peter issued further decrees compelling merchants and nobles to take up residence in his new city. On January 16, 1712 he issued an ukase in which he ordered one thousand gentry, one thousand merchants (half from the "upper," half from the "middle" classes), and one thousand craftsmen (half of whom were required to possess and maintain their own manufacturing facilities) to move to Kotlin Island in the delta of the Neva at the end of the war.[16] On June 3, 1714 another ukase was issued, this time ordering the desirable elements of the country's population to move to St. Petersburg in the following proportions:

1. 350 noblemen, each having over 100 peasants in his possession.
2. 300 merchants from the upper and lower classes.
3. 300 craftsmen from all trades.[17]

The ukase further ordered the construction of 950 additional houses in St. Petersburg which were to be completed during the summer to permit immediate occupancy in the autumn.[18]

The new arrivals found no paradise. The early houses were generally only one story high and modeled after the simple cottage which Peter had built for himself in what he described as "the Prussian manner." The woodwork was frequently painted over to give the appearance of stone of which there was a shortage. The water was foul and in its place the inhabitants consumed quantities of wine, vodka, and beer. Peter himself preferred a beverage consisting of cognac, cayenne, and pepper, a mixture that may have saved him from fatal chills but—as an autopsy showed—played havoc with his constitution.

In addition to these inconveniences the citizens lived in fear of the many thieves and other criminals imported by Peter for forced labor. The streets were so unsafe that at night barricades had to be erected which in turn had to be guarded by hired watchmen. Even worse, palisades had to be built around the houses to keep out the wolves that prowled the streets with the approach of night. Small wonder that the quagmires, floods, prowling criminals and wolves made the city highly unpopular with the Tsar's Muscovite subjects. Quite apart from these discomforts, St. Petersburg seemed alien to all their traditions which revered Kiev and Moscow as truly representative of the Russian spirit and heritage.

Faced by popular discontent and the many concrete obstacles to his plans, Peter ruled harshly and without mercy. The principal squares of St. Petersburg were furnished with gallows and spiked pillars so that anybody who disobeyed orders or opposed imperial policy could immediately be hanged. The iron spikes atop the pillar which stood on Troitski Square often bore the impaled heads of such offenders as well as of ordinary criminals. Not until the reign of Peter II were these ghastly instruments of punishment removed.

In spite of all this the city continued to grow. It is estimated that in 1704 there were 15 houses in St. Petersburg, in 1709 there were 150, and in 1714 as many as 485. Its transformation into a capital city was also a gradual one. Even though Peter called St. Petersburg the capital as early as 1704, the Court, the diplomatic corps, and most of the administrative offices remained in Moscow for almost another decade. The Court did not move to St. Petersburg until 1712, and the Senate, which had been organized in Moscow, was moved to St. Petersburg only in 1713, the year in which the city was officially proclaimed the new capital of Russia. The transfer of the diplomatic corps to the new capital was even more gradual, and was only completed in 1718, while the central administration and its institutions remained in Moscow, as Peter had wished.[19]

Aside from the manner in which the building of St. Petersburg proceeded, namely, as a large scale exercise in absolute royal power, four major factors account for the success of the undertaking.[20]

The first stemmed from the fact that the building of St. Petersburg involved the entire country. In the course of several decades, tens of thousands of craftsmen and workers had been gathered from all ends of the country to toil on the construction of St. Petersburg. At the same time, the remainder of the population was forced to carry a heavy burden of overwhelming additional taxation and other obligations connected with the project. In this sense, the building of St.

Petersburg became the concern of the entire Russian population.[21]

The second factor was the role which private capital and enterprise were called upon to play in augmenting the resources provided by the state. The project was so vast that even a large country like Russia was unable to finance all aspects of it out of the public treasury. Moreover, with the steadily expanding scope of the project, it was necessary to find effective means of assuring the completion of its various phases. Hence, as the direct adjunct of the compulsory settlement of the city—and one of the primary reasons for which it was enforced—private capital was mobilized to assist in the building of St. Petersburg. This was accomplished by obliging the new settlers to build their own residential facilities at their own expense, and by forcing them to maintain the physical plant of the resulting large residential districts.[22]

The third factor was Peter I's successful effort to establish both in St. Petersburg and in the surrounding regions factories which manufactured all types of building materials. This resulted in increased productivity, the teaching of new skills to the local population, and furthermore provided for an almost uninterrupted chain of building activity in and around the city of St. Petersburg.[23]

The fourth and last factor comprised the amount and extent of European knowledge, skill, and experience employed in the construction of St. Petersburg. For Peter was determined to introduce new methods of building as well as new conditions of living into Russia. Thus, as mentioned previously, pre-Petrine cities were characterized by random and uncontrolled growth. With the exception of those in the kremlins, there were very few large city squares. The streets in these old cities were always narrow, crooked, and determined only by the manner in which individual property

Population growth of St. Petersburg (Leningrad) 1703–1966

Approximate figures

1703	date of foundation
1725	70,000
1796	225,000
1825	400,000
1870	660,000
1890	950,000
1900	1,250,000
1913	2,000,000
1940	2,500,000
1966	3,000,000
1974	4,243,000

owners had chosen to build on them. Beginning with St. Petersburg, however, cities were always to be planned, their streets to be straight, wide, paved with stone, and illuminated by street lights. Construction which flanked the streets was heavily regulated. Instead of the kremlin and its fortifications there would be squares or systems of squares which would expand in relation to the city's growth, unite parks, and extend to river embankments.[24] The foreign specialists, invited to Russia by Peter, passed on their knowledge to the Russians, thereby creating a group of qualified native workers and technical personnel well-versed in the technology of that time. Finally, new ways of organizing public services, municipal government, and city management were likewise incorporated.[25]

Peter I died in the early morning of February 8, 1725 of a serious bladder complaint aggravated by a plunge into the ice-cold sea to save the life of some shipwrecked sailors. Thus ended the career of a strange and frightening man.

He was followed by his wife Catherine I, who died in 1727 after a short and uneventful reign. By the time of Peter I's death the population of the capital had reached nearly one hundred thousand (see population chart p. xxvi). His death was followed by a veritable exodus of formerly captive citizens, but this setback was only temporary. Catherine I was followed by Peter II, who disliked St. Petersburg and transferred the government to Moscow. He died of smallpox on the day arranged for his wedding in 1730, without designating a successor.

His death ushered in the so-called "age of the empresses," and also initiated a new phase in the growth and development of St. Petersburg. The empresses were: Anna, Elisabeth, and finally Catherine II (the Great). Their combined rule lasted for sixty years and represents one of the most colorful periods in Russian history. The masculine jollifications of Peter's time gave way to extravagant parties in typical 18th century European style. French wines replaced brandy, and fêtes, theatricals and fireworks displays often lasted for days. It is said that "the frame of St. Petersburg is Peter's, but the gold garlands and colorful decorations are the legacy of the empresses." While the original buildings were mostly of wood and painted plaster, the edifices built during the reign of the empresses were on an immeasurably grander scale and made of stone and marble. Academic classicism, including the tradition of pillars and pediments, was introduced by Catherine, and the city gained symmetry and formality. St. Petersburg was transformed from an outpost at the edge of the empire into a large and elegant metropolis vying in beauty and excitement with the other large cities of the continent.

After Catherine II's death in 1796, her son Paul ascended the throne, but was murdered by his associates in March 1801.

Paul's son, Alexander I, started the "age of the tsars," followed by Nikolai I, Alexander II (who was murdered by revolutionaries in 1881), Alexander III, and finally Nikolai II who was shot by the Bolsheviks in 1918. Only Alexander II's reign was marked by significant contributions to the history of the planning of St. Petersburg (see text). The second half of the 19th century marked the decline of the art of city building in Russia as well as the end of an era of unbelievable extravagance and splendor. War, hunger, and discontent, along with the unsolved problem of serfdom slowly undermined the very foundations of the autocracy. The triumph over Napoleon had not only brought glory to Russia, but had also opened the door to new ideas of constitutional government, freedom and material prosperity. Brutal suppression, strict censorship, and the banishment of revolutionary leaders could not arrest this process.

When World War I broke out in 1914, the whole edifice of the Russian government was shaken to its foundations, culminating in the overthrow of the autocracy by the Russian Revolution. After the revolution, St. Petersburg—now called Leningrad—lost its position as the capital and Moscow again became the first city of this vast country. However, it must be said that St. Petersburg's decline was not solely due to the post-revolutionary transfer of the capital to Moscow. The coming of the railroad in the early 19th century had already begun to change the relationship of St. Petersburg to the rest of Russia and the world. As railroad building progressed, Moscow became more accessible from Europe by train than was St. Petersburg by ship. The construction of the Trans-Siberian Railroad further enhanced Moscow's role by connecting it to the Far East.

In spite of all this, and in spite of damaging developments in the second half of the 18th century and during the 19th century (see text), much of the beauty and majesty of this magnificent city has been preserved to our day. Leningrad today is a thriving manufacturing center with a population of approximately three million, proud of its history, inhabited by a people who by their sacrifice and tenacity have realized one of the most incredible feats in the history of city building.

Part I
THE ENSEMBLE OF ST. PETERSBURG IN THE 18th CENTURY

The theory is frequently advanced that the planning of a city—this or that system of street layout and the general disposition of its other elements—has no substantial bearing on its architectural or aesthetic appearance. The protagonists of this theory claim that, strictly speaking, the plan of a city is there to solve functional problems first. This point of view was to a certain degree expressed even by Camillo Sitte, who said that a city must be called beautiful or ugly regardless of its particular plan.

At first glance there seems to be a good deal of truth in this contention. Many of the cities of ancient Greece and a number of contemporary North American cities have similar basic plans. Despite this the former were characterized by high aesthetic and architectural qualities while quite the opposite holds for many of the latter. On the other hand there are beautiful cities, like Prague and Venice, whose plans as such appear confused and unattractive. And there are other cities whose plans—in terms of planar composition—are attractive on paper, but which, when seen in three dimensions, are not celebrated for their beauty.

In spite of all this the above theory must be considered wrong. The history of urban design shows that planning does indeed predetermine the position and location of the important spaces in a city as well as their mutual architectural and aesthetic interrelationships, thus fixing the character of the general ensemble in a definite way. The best proof of the fallacy of this theory is the planning of St. Petersburg.

1

St. Petersburg in the first quarter of the 18th century

The city, creation of man, changes the natural landscape and its original character forever. Nature, with its changing forms, colors, and moods subsequently re-enters the plan of the city by influencing its architectural character as well as its overall spatial structure. However, the natural features of the site do not by themselves determine the architectural fate of the city. Different periods attach different values to the relationship between the works of man and those of nature. What seems to be of utmost importance in one epoch has little or no significance in another. Nevertheless, there is no doubt that the peculiarities of the site impress their particular seal upon the face of the city, since both share a common fate, and since in some cases the compositional axes and the structural skeleton of the plan are in fact fully determined by these conditions. The Russian architect, I. Zholtovski, remarked on many occasions that nature must be regarded as the final complete whole in all architectural design—including urban design—and that "each project eventually becomes part of this larger entity, and thus is ultimately subordinate to it." [1]

One may dispute the absolute necessity of subordinating each and every architectural ensemble to the existing condition of the site, but it is equally difficult to ignore the fact that landscape has an important part to play in the architectural development of a city.

Let us therefore examine the character and appearance of the territory on which the new capital of Russia—St. Petersburg—was founded in 1703.[2] One may also ask how the architectural organization of the city was influenced by the natural features of the site, especially during the first decade of its existence.

The delta of the Neva River is generally flat and plain, with an almost imperceptible slope descending toward the sea.[3] Since the vegetation that covered almost all of the land area of the marshy site was scant, it did not have to be taken into account in the planning of the city. Consequently, as neither land formation nor plant cover was of any decisive importance during the initial planning stages, the only important elements that did have to be taken into account were: the river, the bay, and the natural configuration of the shorelines of the land masses in the delta of the Neva. The site was furthermore traversed by a network of numerous winding streams and rivulets which formed the delta and which entered the bay along the broad waterfront of the many separate islands (see illustration 1).

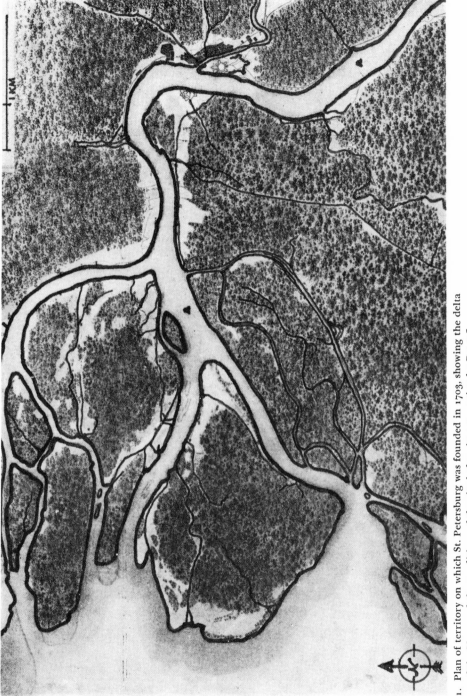

1. Plan of territory on which St. Petersburg was founded in 1703, showing the delta of the Neva and the conditions of the site before its occupation by Peter I.

On May 1, 1703, the armies of Peter I captured the Swedish fortress of Nienschanz, left half-destroyed by the siege. With the capture of this fortress Russia finally gained access to the Baltic Sea. After defeating the Swedes, it was necessary to secure the conquered territory.

Three days before the final assault, Peter I had taken seven companies of his Guards and descended downstream along the Neva, measuring the depth of the river for future navigation. The results of these measurements proved that seagoing vessels could proceed upstream only via the Bolshaia Neva (the large branch of the Neva). The deep draught passed below the shore of Vasilevskii Ostrov (Vasilevski Island) [4] subsequently shifting in the direction of the present Admiralteiskaia Storona (the Admiralty District) near the Strelka (cape) [5] of Vasilevski Island. This knowledge became very important in the selection of the site for the Peter and Paul Fortress and also for future development of the city itself. [6]

In order to protect the newly conquered territory it was first of all necessary to block the estuaries of the Neva. For this purpose fortifications had to be erected to prevent enemy ships from entering and proceeding up the river. The selection of the site for the new fortress was left to a military council. This council also discussed the future location of the city and the reconstruction of the fortifications which were to replace the conquered Swedish ones. Since the Neva was navigable only along its larger branch, the fortress was finally built lower downstream in its present location (see illustration 2) and the old Swedish fortifications were abandoned.

Not only did this choice satisfy the military and defense needs of the moment but it also served to enhance the future architectural and aesthetic character of the city. Moreover, from the viewpoint of natural orientation the new site for the fortress was considerably more advantageous than that of the

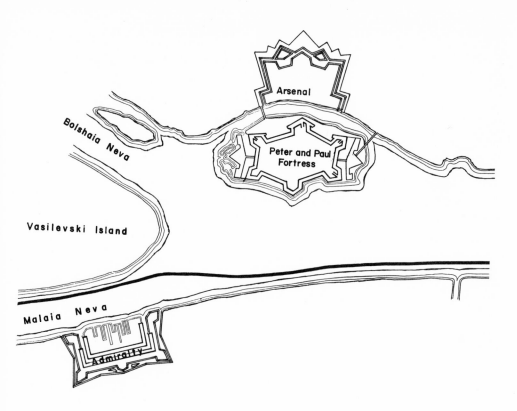

2. Schematic drawing showing the Peter and Paul Fortress, the Admiralty Fortress; the heavy black line indicates the navigation channel of the Neva.

old Swedish fort near the mouth of the Okhta. And as far as natural beauty was concerned the territory chosen for the new center of the city occupied the best available location within the Neva delta. The spatial and architectural elements of the city center were thus brought into juxtaposition with the large expanses of surrounding water surfaces. These were the factors that determined the mutual scale relationships of the central ensemble of St. Petersburg in the 18th century. In 1704 it was decided to move the Admiralty to St. Petersburg because of the many difficulties connected with the transfer of newly built vessels from Lake Ladoga to the Gulf of Finland. In the selection of a site for the Admiralty, the navigable depth of the river once again became the determining factor. The Admiralty itself was designed for a dual purpose, to serve as a shipbuilding wharf on the one hand and as a second fortress protecting the Neva estuaries on the other. The site chosen for the complex was opposite and slightly below the Strelka of Vasilevski Island (see illustration 2). By virtue of this highly strategic location the Neva was now covered by cannons from both sides, making it virtually impossible for the enemy to penetrate inland by ship.

The location of the Admiralty in many ways predetermined the future planning of the central part of the city—later called the Admiralty District of St. Petersburg.[7] This particular territory is defined on one side by the Neva and on the other by the Fontanka. In form it resembles a drawn bow, with the Admiralty occupying the place of the arrow-tail. Within the limits described by the Fontanka the Admiralty divides the waterfront into two almost equal parts later called Dvortsovaia Naberezhnaia (Palace Quay) and Angliiskaia Naberezhnaia (English Quay). The Admiralty is thus in the geometrical center of two concentric semicircles, outlined by the rivers Fontanka and Moika, and occupies the center of a compositional situation which owes much to the disposition of the natural features of the site itself.

The location of the two fortresses was therefore primarily a consequence of strategic considerations, though it eventually proved to be an architectural asset as well. The spatial juxtaposition of these two elements became the most important factor affecting the planning of St. Petersburg in the first decade of its existence.

The actual transfer of the capital from Moscow to St. Petersburg took place in the years 1709–12. The transformation of a military outpost into a capital city confronted the planners with new problems which went beyond the initial requirements of strategic location and defense. The function of the fortress city had to be broadened to include all the other features of a normal city. Besides being a fortress, it also had to serve as a harbor and as the seat of the national government. Apart from these functional requirements, the aesthetic element also had to be considered, since Peter I wanted this city to become the "show window" of the Russian Empire. Thus, in the first quarter of the 18th century the architect-planners were faced with two basic tasks. First, they had to design and erect mass housing to relieve the acute shortage of accommodations, a problem which they solved by means of so-called "model projects" (see illustration 3). Secondly, they had to plan the construction of a "prestige center" along the shores of the Neva between its estuary and the present Vyborg District.

Most of the palaces and important government buildings were located along the Neva waterfront. The commercial harbor found its location on the Strelka of Vasilevski Island. Alongside the harbor rose the buildings of the Twelve Colleges, the Kunstkammer[8] and also the palace of the all-powerful Count Alexander Menshikov. The central part of the city was at that time taken up by the Peter and Paul Fortress. At approximately the same time the various palaces of the Tsar's favorites were being built on the south shore of the Neva above the Admiralty Building. Peter built his own residence—the so-called first Winter Palace—near the just completed Zimnaia Kanavka (Small Winter Canal) to the east of which the Letnii Sad (Summer Garden) was laid out.

This new "face" of the city was above all calculated to impress foreign visitors approaching the harbor and Strelka of Vasilevski Island from the direction of the Gulf of Finland. The courts, the stores, the Gostinyi Dvor (Bazaar)[9] and the Exchange were located on the side of the Malaia Neva

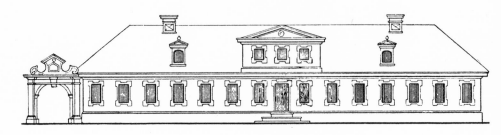

1 0 1 2 3 4 5 6 7 8 м

1 0 1 2 3 4 5 м

3. Top: So-called "model houses" along the shores of Vasilevski Island in the western region of the Bolshaia Neva. Bottom: So-called "model houses with cellars" along the shores of the Moika (Trezzini's design).

(the small branch of the Neva). As soon as incoming ships rounded the tip of Vasilevski Island passengers could see the whole panorama of the rapidly growing city unfolding before their eyes. The Strelka was in fact the best spot from which to view the new capital of Russia. Peter I was well aware of the likelihood that sailors and merchants visiting St. Petersburg would soon spread the news of its phenomenal growth and magnificence throughout Europe. Thus architectural means were used to further a political purpose.

The internal life of this part of St. Petersburg was vibrant with many activities, including the construction of buildings, shipbuilding, and the teaching of navigation. It was also the site of festivals and fireworks. The waterfront was not only the show window of the capital but also the economic base of its existence. Concurrently with actual construction went the paper planning of the new Russian capital.

On June 19, 1716, during a trip from Paris to St. Petersburg, Peter I met Jean Baptiste Alexander Leblond [10] in Piermont, and subsequently spent three full days in conversation with him. It is not known what was said during these conversations between the Tsar and the future chief architect of St. Petersburg. But the following lines in an introductory letter which Peter gave Leblond to take to Count Menshikov give an indication of what went on:

> This master possesses extraordinary qualities and great talent, as I could readily observe in a short time. . . . Therefore, all architects [in St. Petersburg] shall be informed that no future construction shall be commenced without his signature being affixed to the plans, including projects already started, provided that they can still be corrected.[11]

In August of the same year, Leblond took on the duties of chief architect of St. Petersburg, thus embarking upon a short but very fruitful career in that city. By that time St. Peters-

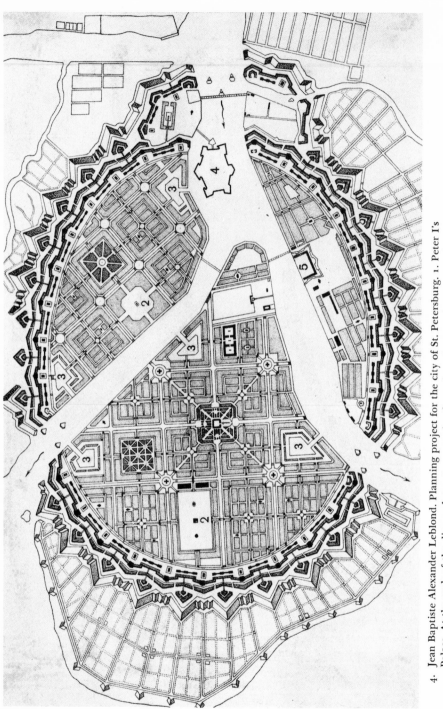

4. Jean Baptiste Alexander Leblond. Planning project for the city of St. Petersburg. 1. Peter I's Palace. At the ends of the diagonal streets emanating from the palace are four squares with cathedral churches at the center, indicated by black crosses; 2. Market squares; 3. Harbors with storage houses; 4. Peter and Paul Fortress; 5. Admiralty.

burg had already grown considerably, especially along the shores of the Neva. Around the Peter and Paul Fortress, on Gorodski Island, around the old Admiralty, and within the Admiralty District itself considerable construction was under way. One of the first documents connected with Leblond's name is his memorandum to Peter I: *Concerning the poor construction practices prevalent in the city of St. Petersburg.*[12]

On January 7, 1717, Leblond finished his famous plan for the city of St. Petersburg. According to a caption on the plan it was put together "in great haste, during a period of four days." It shows St. Petersburg placed in the central part of the Neva delta surrounded by a ring of fortifications—not unlike a spiky porcupine. At this time the defense of the river approaches from the Gulf of Finland was considered to be the city's most important function. Swedish warships still controlled the Baltic Sea, and the possibility of attack could as yet not be discounted. Leblond proposed the creation of a three-tiered system of fortifications to form a protective oval around the central part of the city (see illustration 4). Apart from its strategic significance the Gulf of Finland obviously also greatly influenced the general configuration of the architectural plan of the city.[13]

As the war with Sweden came to an end, the significance of the city as a fortress declined, and more attention was given to its architectural development. During the early years of its existence St. Petersburg gradually transformed itself from a small fortress at the periphery of the empire into a large capital city.

Illustration 5 shows the land formations oriented toward the bay. These generate a system of "natural" axes, marked A-A', and perpendicular to it the axis B-B'. Leblond's axes are shown hatched, and marked C-C'. The axis A-A' represents a nearly perfect bisection of the bay and the delta. The second

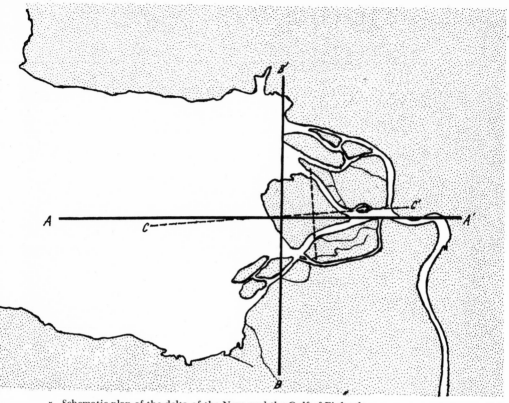

5. Schematic plan of the delta of the Neva and the Gulf of Finland
showing the so-called "natural" axes in heavy black lines (A-A')
and Leblond's compositional axes hatched (C-C').

axis, B-B', passes through the east shore of the bay, where
numerous little islands project into the sea. Such a system of
natural axes offers the possibility of a great number of architectural solutions for the city and the surrounding area. Leblond was the first architect-planner to see this. His system of
major axes coincides very closely with that of the "natural"
ones. In the scheme the long arm A-A' bisects the Gulf of
Finland and the shorter one, B-B', passes the lower part of
the eastern shoreline, drawing it within the architectural
sphere of influence of the central composition. This is the
first and most successful feature of Leblond's proposal.

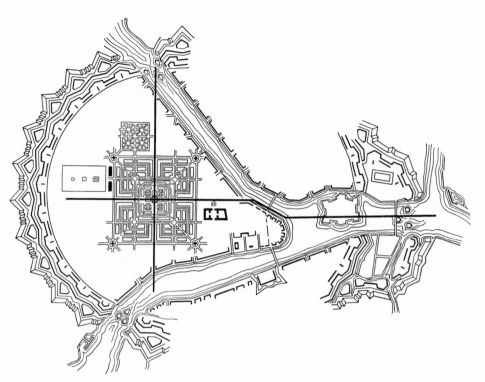

6. A fragment of Leblond's plan, showing the most important architectural elements of the city.

A study of illustration 6 reveals that the long axis of the fortification oval and that of the central composition do not coincide. It is questionable that Leblond would have permitted such a shift of axes without some important reason. It may be that he did so because he incorporated parts of the existing fortifications into the geometry of his new fortification system.[14] This shift of axes compounded the complexity of his scheme, adding an element of dynamism to the static form of the oval in the direction of the bay. The axiality of the city plan architecturally defined Vasilevski Island as the center of the capital. The regularly spaced elements of the oval ring of fortifications surrounding the city found their architectural counterpoint in the water surface of the bay. From there one could also see, rising above the walls, the most significant structures of the city. Leblond's plan for St. Petersburg was thus oriented toward the Gulf of Finland. The low belt of fortification walls, the mouths of the big cannons, the long lines of barracks, the two watergates at the estuaries of the Neva, and rising above all else the large watchtowers—all of this seen together would have offered an impressive sight to anyone approaching the new capital through the Baltic fog.

Leblond proposed a trisectional fortification system, separated by the estuaries of the Neva. The walls were arranged in tiers of varying height descending toward the sea. The placement of cannons on all of the tiers would have brought about a considerable increase in firepower. For the interior of the city Leblond proposed a complete system of canals. A network of sluices and canals divided the fortifications into various zones "which could be flooded in case of attack, thus forcing the enemy into quick retreat." [15] The exterior appearance of the fortification walls reflected their multilevel design, with each succeeding plane rising above the previous one, and the whole finally crowned by a ring of barracks and powder magazines. The regular spacing of the projecting bastions was determined by military considerations. It became the most characteristic feature of the exterior of the enclosing fortification walls. The bastions—thrusting outward and facing each other at the same time—would have produced an awe-inspiring, fascinating picture. The architectural organization of the fortification walls would have given a unified expression to the whole waterfront which then, as now, appeared rather chaotic. This is the second most successful feature of Leblond's proposal.

Certain critics of Leblond's design assume that his architectural center of St. Petersburg consisted of Peter I's palace and its immediate surroundings only, all arranged within a square, with a cathedral at each of the four corners (see illustration 6). This view is not quite correct. It presupposes only one function for the city, namely, that of imperial capital. But in fact St. Petersburg was already at that time a busy seaport and fortress as well as the capital of Russia. Not even Peter I and his court ever regarded the administrative quarter as the most important part of the city. On the contrary, defense and trade were considered the most significant factors in the development of the growing capital. Peter I's awareness of the strategic and commercial importance of the city is reflected in his ukase dividing its territory as follows: Admiralty Island along the Neva for shipbuilding and the fleet; Gorodski Island (i.e., the St. Petersburg District) for tradesmen; and Vasilevski Island for the buildings of the court, the trade port, and trade in general.[16] To imagine a city center locked within the confines of Vasilevski Island and unrelated to the other territories is to misunderstand the full implications of Leblond's design.

The most important visual aspect of the city was its silhouette as seen from the Gulf of Finland. The architectural task of planning the city center in such a way as to make it significant within the total skyline was a major one. Leblond used several devices to achieve this. His plan proposed three major water entrances to the city, one from the Upper Neva and two from the bay. These represented the "city gates." The Bolshaia Neva and the Malaia Neva, together with their shorelines, served as the principal thoroughfares of the city. The shorelines became important spatial elements, determining to a large degree the architectural setting of the city within the landscape.

The harbor at the tip of Vasilevski Island reinforced the significance of the shorelines as an architecturally determining feature. At that time the harbor represented the focal point in the life of the city.

Within the very mouth of the Malaia Neva, Leblond placed three water bastions, "each equipped with ten cannons," to protect the river approaches from attack. Behind those, to the right and the left, were the entrances to the harbor, and facilities "for the importation of food stuffs." [17] Farther back were rows of dwellings, separated by numerous canals and bridges. The architectural expression of the waterfront was based on contrast. Behind the large and powerful fortifications, and after passing the bastions, the visitor would have found modest buildings laid out in an orderly manner. The comparatively small size of the actual building lots further contributed to this scaling down of building size. The regular interruption of the shorelines by a network of canals would have emphasized the contrast between the island character of the land mass and the surrounding waterways. This would have been especially apparent near the Strelka. The plan indicates that the canals of Vasilevski Island were to enter at an angle to the shorelines, facilitating the visual penetration of the whole territory. Thus, Peter I's palace could have been glimpsed alongside the first canal, confirming the fact that Vasilevski Island is spatially more important than Gorodski Island.

The next most important element of the plan is the central part of Vasilevski Island, which consists of Peter I's palace and the adjacent spaces. As mentioned earlier the palace was merely one of many elements in the spatial system of Leblond's planning proposal. Considering the large area covered, the many diverse elements surrounding the palace, and the overall complexity of the plan, one can easily understand that one single building could not by itself become the architectural center of such a large city. Only a larger system of spaces and volumes could have solved this problem. A study of Leblond's plan reveals that the architectural influence of the palace would have been confined to the space of the central square and would have found its formal termination in the four corners, where cathedrals were to be located. Adjacent to the central square, Leblond proposed a park and a large square in the manner of a Place d'Armes. In terms of structural organization these can be regarded as independent spaces. They have their own axes of symmetry and Leblond treated them as independent design elements. They were to be fused into a coherent whole with the rest of the design only by the general organization of the spatial structure of the plan. Within the limits of the central square, all elements were arranged in such a way as to underline the central importance of the palace. The spatial importance of the palace was emphasized by the square park surrounding it, while directional emphasis was provided by the diagonal streets emanating from the four corners to the outer square.

The whole concept was based on a system of two perpendicular axes. The short axis was subordinated in importance to the long, major axis. Along the latter the following spaces were to be located: the "armed camp," a parade ground 140m x 280m (460 ft. x 920 ft.) in size together with a statue of "His Majesty on foot," a large tower which was to serve as an observation post, and finally a "triumphal column." The main axis of the scheme then passes through the central quarters, the park, and the palace. Behind the central quarters the Academy of Sciences joins the axis and, touching Menshikov Park, finally exits toward the Malaia Neva. Its point of exit appears arbitrary, for it would have been much more logical to let it pass through the Strelka of Vasilevski Island. One of the most plausible explanations for this curious deflection of the main axis is the fact that it would otherwise have cut in half the properties of the all-powerful Count Menshikov—something he would not have permitted for any reason whatsoever.

We are thus confronted by a complex architectural composition. On the one hand there is the panorama of the town —the quays, the gates, and the Peter and Paul Fortress: on the other the more or less independent town center lodged in the interior of Vasilevski Island. This apparent spatial isolation of the palace from the Neva waterfront must be regarded as the principal weakness of Leblond's design.

Leblond's scheme was never realized. In fact, nothing at all was done according to his plan. Historians explain this in several ways. Of the various theories mentioned the following are the most plausible. One has it that the project was blocked by the intrigues of Count Menshikov and his followers. The other contends that the proposal was beyond the technical means at the disposal of the Russians in the early 18th century. Of these two theories, the latter appears to be the more probable one. Leblond's vast scheme was certainly almost impossible to achieve given Russia's economic potential at that time. He proposed to raise the whole base of the city by placing all buildings upon an additional layer of earth to be obtained from the canal excavations. Without this device it would have been impossible to build in the western part of Vasilevski Island due to the constant danger of flooding. Obviously such an undertaking could have been financed only by the government. Peter I at that time had neither the financial nor the technical resources to realize such a grandiose project.

Leblond's plan, conceived "in great haste" in four days, was one of the most significant planning projects for the Russian capital in the first quarter of the 18th century, but it was not the only one. There is no doubt, however, that it was based on the best planning concepts of that time. Let us therefore

7. An etching made by
I. B. Homann in 1716,
showing Trezzini's
planning project for
Vasilevski Island.

examine how the future planning of the city was influenced by his ideas and how fruitful these proved to be in the long run.

The planning and development of Vasilevski Island as the central region of the capital was already under consideration in 1714, and two architects—Domenico Trezzini [18] and Gerbel (see illustration 7)—were commissioned to prepare plans for this area. By the time Leblond arrived in St. Petersburg, both had already worked out their own proposals and Peter I's endorsement: "Petersburg—to be built according to this plan" had been secured for one of these. As chief architect, Leblond was expected either to continue with the existing plan or to disagree with it. Being new on the job, and not wanting to be surrounded by a hostile group of collaborators, he refrained from criticism, at least in the beginning. In his memorandum to Peter I, *Concerning the poor construction practices prevalent in the city of St. Petersburg,* he also spoke his mind on the subject of the spatial and architectural organization of the capital. Although these notes became the basis for his later planning proposal, he did not at this point become involved with the actual planning of the city. At the beginning of 1717 Matarnovi prepared a new plan essentially based on a design by Trezzini. It was in response to this proposal that Leblond submitted his scheme, and it was for this reason that it was prepared "in great haste." All drawings and proposals, together with other "matters of state," had to be dispatched by courier, since the Tsar was abroad at the time. To ensure that his project would be considered with the others Leblond had to work with great speed.

In the projects drawn up by Trezzini, Matarnovi, and Gerbel, Vasilevski Island was visually separated from all the other parts of the city. Its circumference was made up by a ring of flat, low buildings, and its interior was cut up by a series of mutually perpendicular canals. The authors of these schemes completely ignored the surrounding landscape and the structure of the existing city. The building blocks were laid out in a dull, mechanical manner, without any architectural center or focus. The existing layout of Vasilevski Island is the product of these proposals. Judged by both aesthetic and architectural criteria, Leblond's scheme was vastly superior.

Leblond obviously had to take into account to some degree the prior proposals prepared by Trezzini, Matarnovi, and Gerbel, especially since one of these had already been approved by the Tsar. Furthermore it was Peter's idea to drain the swamps of St. Petersburg by means of canals, and even the chief architect was powerless against the iron will of the Tsar.

Before leaving Paris to fill the post of chief architect of St. Petersburg, Leblond in all likelihood studied most of the significant planning projects being undertaken in the second half of the 17th century, especially those in France and the Scandinavian countries, as well as some in other places which resembled St. Petersburg in their general topographical features. During the latter part of the 17th century the art of city planning in France was characterized by large residence complexes such as Versailles and by large city fortresses, many of which were newly built or rebuilt by Marshal Vauban. These plans were based on ideal geometrical shapes which were at the same time functionally adapted to the requirements of defense. Many of the contemporary planning projects then being realized in Holland and in Scandinavia shared various features with St. Petersburg, such as their location near the sea or within the delta of a river. One example is the new plan of Amsterdam, published in 1662. This includes regular blocks, a widened port, and a new system of peripheral bastions, describing a wide semicircle around the city. In 1683, Erik Dahlberg had proposed a plan for the Swedish city of Karlskrone with a brilliant combination of defense works and water areas. In 1690, the new plan for Copenhagen had been published. This shows the city surrounded by a continuous circle of bastions with a beautiful star-shaped citadel inside.

Certainly Peter I himself was quite familiar with city planning developments in Western Europe, either by personal observation or by study. Leblond's project was clearly based on these principles, although he succeeded in surpassing many of them in the quality of his architectural conception. But although there are certain general similarities between Leblond's plan and those for Venice and Amsterdam, a careful comparison reveals that this similarity is superficial and mainly due to the location of all three cities near the sea and the presence of numerous canals. Undoubtedly Peter's well-known admiration of Amsterdam and his repeated admonitions to his architects to follow the "manner of the Dutch" also influenced Leblond.

Theories have been advanced that Leblond's design was inspired by drawings of "ideal cities" of the Renaissance. There is little doubt that Leblond was familiar with the plans of the "ideal cities" of the Italian Renaissance and that he recognized their fundamental simplicity and geometry. One may further assume that he utilized these basic concepts in his own work, but a careful comparison shows that his design is of an infinitely more complex nature, owing to the subtle spatial relationships among its individual components. In addition to the foregoing there is also a definite similarity between certain details of Leblond's plan and the geometrical designs of Vasari and Dilich-Schäffer.[19] But again it would be difficult to discover in these the variety and spatial complexity within a basically clear and simple geometrical framework, so characteristic of Leblond's plan of St. Petersburg. All of these features of his plan were a direct response and presented a viable architectural solution to the problems posed by the actual situation.

A comparison of Leblond's plan with the layout of Amsterdam and Venice is equally difficult and inconclusive. It shows that the architectural organization and the functional purpose of the waterways are fundamentally different in each case. The radial-concentric system of Amsterdam and the picturesque layout of Venice could hardly have been the model for Leblond's clear and precise geometrical plan for St. Petersburg. Leblond, a French architect, was a pupil of LeNotre. He was a rationalist and a protagonist of regular and ordered planning methods, skeptical of anything that gave the appearance of being random or accidental and not subject to logical analysis. The nature of his task was essentially defined by the needs of his age and was probably formulated during those few days in Piermont, when the future chief architect met Peter I for the first time.

If any definite sources of inspiration are to be considered at all, one should include: the fortifications of the French castles of the 17th century, the planning achievements of Scandinavia, and finally, the plan of Versailles. These seem to have been the basic sources of Leblond's plan for the center of St. Petersburg.

Although the plan was never realized, its influence upon the further development of Russian city planning should not be underestimated. This is especially true for Russian planning in the 18th century. The expressionless and mediocre projects of Trezzini, Gerbel, and Matarnovi were vastly inferior to Leblond's design. His scheme was the only one which gave architectural expression to the importance of the new Russian capital. Its main virtues lay in its conceptual clarity and overall unity. At the same time it symbolized man's conquest of formless nature by means of conceptual precision and by recognition and use of the implied major natural axes to support the basic geometrical logic and the conceptual order of the plan.

2

The "three prongs" of St. Petersburg

In spite of all of Peter's efforts and in spite of his numerous and cruel ukases the city center of St. Petersburg did not develop on Vasilevski Island. There were two chief reasons for this: first, its physical separation from the mainland, and second, its very low ground level which made it vulnerable to frequent flooding. Another important factor was the development of the Admiralty District on the opposite shore. The Winter Palace and most of the official residences were located there. Peter I was continually absent, and during his short visits to St. Petersburg contented himself with short and random inspections of individual projects. For official receptions and audiences he used the Menshikov Palace; mainly because at that time it was the most imposing building in the whole city. Councils and official meetings were often held in the palaces of his court, since there were no suitable facilities in his own residence. For his personal use he maintained a small house on the Petersburg side and sometimes stayed at the Summer Palace. He kept another house on Dvortsovaia Quay, which he set up with the "permission of the Admiralty" as "master of naval sciences." At any rate, an official court "in keeping with the grandeur of His Imperial Highness" did not exist in St. Petersburg at that time. The present Winter Palace was built much later.

Soon after the completion of the original Admiralty Building and in the approximate location of the present Winter Palace various palaces were built for members of the royal family, the courtiers, and the nobility, most of whom were in one way or another connected with shipbuilding and naval affairs. One of these courtiers, Count Apraksin, who left no heir, willed his Petersburg residence to Peter II. The house of Apraksin occupied the front of the lot which was later built over by Rastrelli. It faced the Neva on one side and the Admiralty on the other. During his short reign (1727–30), Peter II spent most of his time in Moscow and did not use the house of Apraksin, but his successor, Anna Ivanovna (1730–40), converted it into her personal town residence, the so-called Winter Palace. From 1736 onward the palace was remodeled and enlarged by annual additions, alterations, and the adaptation of adjacent buildings for additional apartments and service functions. Properties adjacent to the palace were either bought out or simply confiscated.

The selection of this area as the site for the residences of the Russian nobility had far-reaching consequences for the development of the future city center and to a large degree determined the spatial significance of the Admiralty as the architectural focus of the whole area.

After the establishment of the Winter Palace, the actual replanning of this part of the city was started. In Peter I's time the Admiralty District—or more precisely, that part of Admiralty Island situated between the Neva and Glukhoi Protok [1]—was covered by a number of suburbs, including Morskaia, Grecheskaia, Novaia, and Perevedenskaia Sloboda [2] which were not in keeping with the splendor of the newly emerging city center. Together with the palaces and other governmental buildings, the center of the city had now shifted to this new location. Obviously it was undesirable to have such poor neighborhoods in the vicinity of the city center. Most of the properties within these suburbs belonged to citizens whom Peter I had commanded to settle in St. Petersburg to be at the service of the court. There being already considerable discontent among this group, outright confiscation was considered unwise, as it would have precipitated additional unrest or even riots. Apart from these considerations, Peter's ukases and territorial allotments were still in force and none of his successors dared openly to renounce any of his actions.

Although the precise details of the clandestine efforts to solve this problem were never uncovered, their results were predictable. Some evil-tongued historians speak of arson, claiming that the large fires of 1736 and 1737 were started by elements who wanted to incite the population against the government. Whether this was true, nobody knows. However, as a result of these fires, the one and two story wooden structures in the area were destroyed with remarkably methodical speed and precision. The first conflagration cleared the area from the Winter Palace toward the Moika as far as the Kriukov Canal, while the second fire spread along the waterfront and Millionnaia Street all the way to Tsaritsyn Field and the Koniushenov Bridge. On both occasions, the palace and adjoining Lugovaia Street somehow happened to be on the safe side of the wind.

After the second conflagration a number of laws were passed preventing the re-establishment of the old suburbs in the burned-out area. The police director submitted a report to the Cabinet, recommending the relocation of the remaining substandard structures as well as the removal of all blacksmiths, candlestores, and other odious trades from the Admiralty District. The report was approved, and four days after the second fire a royal decree was issued permitting only stone structures with proper masonry foundations to be built in the Admiralty area. The existing owners, mostly small tradesmen, builders, and shipbuilders, could not afford the high cost of stone construction and were thus obliged to move to other parts of the city. At the same time Empress Anna established a new rule denying accommodations in the royal palace to any of her courtiers. All this gave rise to considerable building activity because numerous new residences had to be provided for the many people who were in one way or another attached to the royal court. At the same time a number of new ukases were issued ordering the removal from Admiralty Island of all wooden structures located next to stone buildings. The displaced owners were moved to Vasilevski Island, the Petersburg District, and the Vyborg District. The Admiralty District thus became the place of residence for the court and the aristocracy.

In June, 1737, a Commission for the Orderly Development of St. Petersburg was established [3] and entrusted with the planning of the central part of the city. Peter Eropkin, an architect, was appointed to head this commission which included, among others, Michael Zemtsov [4] and Ivan Korobov, the designer of the new Admiralty. These were the architects who established the system of the "three prongs," i.e., the three radials which converge at the Admiralty.

The design and execution of the system of the "three prongs" did not come about at once, but was achieved gradually and in various stages. Nevski Prospect [5] was laid out first, between 1712 and 1718 (see illustration 8). It connected the center of the city and its most prominent building, the Admiralty, with the old Novgorod Road at the periphery.[6]

As its first order of business the commission ordered the preparation of a topographical map of the city. Known as the Sigheim Plan this became the first map to be based on an actual survey of the territory conducted with the use of surveying instruments. The commission's first planning proposals were then transferred to this map and submitted for approval in December, 1737. The Sigheim Plan, like most 18th century maps was not only a topographical map of the city but to a certain degree a planning tool as well.

Next the commission prepared a detailed proposal for the creation of the "three prongs." The scheme was presented to the Empress Anna I in April, 1738. In this document it was proposed to extend the central avenue, called Gorokhovaia Street (street of nuts) [7] from the Moika to the Fontanka by crossing Perevedenskaia Street, the Novaia Suburb and the properties of Count Apraksin. Beyond the Fontanka, the street was to continue through the properties of the foreigners Evens and Elmsel to connect with the then emerging Zagorodnaia Street. Quite obviously Gorokhovaia Street between Admiralty Field and the Moika was already in existence at that time. This fact is further borne out by the construction of the Krasnyi Bridge across the Moika in 1736.

The future Voznesenski Prospect was at that time already included in the commission's plans. However, one may as-

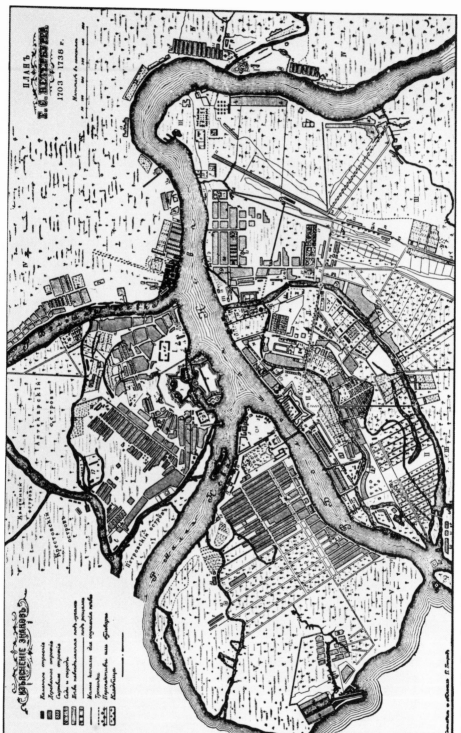

8. Plan of St. Petersburg (1703–1738).

sume that the avenues were not as straight as shown on any of the plans issued between 1718 and 1725. Most maps produced during the reign of Peter I were made without the help of surveying instruments.[8] Other documents, including a directive dated May 20, 1715, and signed by Peter I, attest to the fact that the radials were planned with an orientation toward the Admiralty from the very beginning. The concept of the "three prongs" thus had its origin in Peter I's time. In a collection of *Historical Plans of St. Petersburg*,[9] Tsilov discovered a map dated 1725 which shows two of the radials as already existing.

In the mid-1730's both Voznesenski Prospect and Gorokhovaia Street were still in a rather incomplete state and the commission had to take up the task of redirecting them. In 1738 it was decided to straighten Voznesenski Prospect and Gorokhovaia Street. Thus the "three prongs," conceived and started during Peter's reign and further developed in 1737 to 1738, passed the test of time and secured the full approval of such masters of city planning as Eropkin, Korobov, and Zemtsov. It is doubtful that the system would have survived if it had not conformed to both the needs and the aesthetic tastes of the time. Apart from its functional significance in connecting the old Novgorod Road with the center of the city, Nevski Prospect—already in Peter I's time—provided strong visual support for the view toward the Alexander Nevski Monastery, at that time the architectural symbol of the authority of the capital's clergy.

Shortly after the extension of Voznesenski Prospect and Gorokhovaia Street the Ismailovski and Semenovski Regiments of the Guards were stationed near their terminal points. The Guards represented the chief military support of the monarchy and their proper accommodation was of great concern to the establishment. In the planning of the new center of St. Petersburg special attention had to be paid to the needs of these regiments. In 1738 the Commission for the Orderly Development of St. Petersburg drafted a resolution in which it was proposed to locate these two regiments beyond the Fontanka, at the terminus of the two newly laid out avenues, and in August 1739 detailed plans for the regimental territories were drawn up. At the same time bridges were built across the Moika and Glukhoi Inlet (later the Ekaterinski Canal and now the Griboedov Canal), making it possible for the troops to reach the Winter Palace in the shortest possible time in the event of an emergency.

After the master plan for regimental accommodations had been submitted for approval, one important change was made: instead of ordinary barracks, regular housing was to be provided for both the soldiers and their families. This system of regimental settlement was finally approved in 1739 and, as a result, considerably more land was required than had at first been anticipated. These military suburbs were laid out in a rigid gridiron pattern, entering the plan of the city as unrelated fragments. They were to be completed by the end of 1740 "with the utmost possible speed." Due to a shortage of funds, however, work progressed slowly and it was not until the second half of the 18th century that the regimental quarters were actually finished.

The use of radials as an architectural element preceded the founding of St. Petersburg by several centuries—being evident in the planning of Rome in the first half of the 16th century. The second significant application of this particular system on a large scale is to be found in Versailles.

The radials of Rome represent an architecturally defined "gate" to the city. As the visitor enters the city through the gate of the ancient Aurelian Wall, the large Piazza del Popolo opens before him. The three radials fan out from the piazza toward the city. The right one—Via di Ripetta—leads to Mars Field, the Pantheon, and Piazza Navona; the central one—Via del Corso—leads toward the Capitol, the Colosseum, and the ancient fora; and the left one—Via del Babuino—leads to the Spanish Steps and the Quirinale. The entrance to the central radial street is articulated by two flanking churches. The main feature of the Roman system of radials is the creation of visual perspectives from the exterior of the city toward the important spaces in the interior.

The layout of the Versailles radials represents the antithesis of the Roman system. Starting from separate and spatially unrelated points, the three radials ultimately converge upon the royal palace. However, the geometrical point of their convergence is not articulated and each individual radial has its own visual terminus. The architectural significance of this scheme consists in the centripetal visual movement toward one single complex—the palace. The spatial relationships, the details of the system, and the evolution of the St. Petersburg radials gave them a unique character, especially when compared to the two examples described below.

In Versailles the radials change into suburban streets and are not connected with one another. In St. Petersburg, due chiefly to natural conditions but also as a result of conscious planning, the radials are interconnected by semicircular elements which take the form of streets or canals. Owing to this system of semicircular "ties," the St. Petersburg radials—in contrast to Versailles—are not only unified by the central focal point but also by the numerous transverse elements within the structure of the city. The importance of the Admiralty as a terminating element is thereby enormously increased. Looking along the perspectives of the radials from the interior of Admiralty Island, one can literally almost feel the "directional pull" of the Admiralty Tower. It terminates the perspective of the radials; it rises unexpectedly when one traverses one of the many circular side streets; and it can be glimpsed while one walks along the Moika, the Fontanka, or the Ekaterinski Canal. The tower with its graceful spire is ever present and its importance in the visual organization of the city cannot be overestimated. It provides a constant visual anchor in the orientation of the city. Even from a great distance, when it almost seems to disappear at the end of the long perspectives of both the Nevski and the Voznesenski Prospects, it retains its function as a visual "magnet." The "three prongs" of St. Petersburg thus combine the best features of the radial systems of Versailles and Rome. From Versailles it derives the principle of directional pull from the periphery toward the center; from Rome, the definition of the radials by important complexes along their length. However, there is one important difference between Rome and St. Petersburg. The radials of Rome lead to the eternal monuments of that city, while St. Petersburg has failed to solve the problem of their peripheral termination.

Apart from the latter defect, the "three prongs" of St. Petersburg have always been one of the most successful features of its plan. Despite the many mistakes made during the 19th and 20th centuries and despite the construction of a number of faceless buildings marring their overall architectural unity, the radials have survived and remain the strongest directional elements in the structure of the city. Their ability to withstand the changing forces of time and fashion demonstrates the strength of this planning concept, especially if one considers the fact that even major blunders by insensitive architects could not destroy their basic structural and spatial integrity. The three prongs" of St. Petersburg are thus an exquisite example of the enduring strength of good urban planning.

The establishment of a system of radials poses the question of their effect upon the overall spatial structure of the city. First and most important is the fact that all future planning within the Admiralty District was predetermined by the basic geometry and the spatial structure of the "three prongs," which obviously also included the quays of the Neva, the Moika, Glukhoi Inlet, and the Fontanka. As far as individual architectural building parcels are concerned, the system tends to generate only those buildings which are in harmony with its particular geometry.

In the second place, the radials give formal expression to the civic importance of the Admiralty and the adjacent territory. As a result of all these factors, the Admiralty became the main architectural focus of the whole Admiralty District which in turn developed into the actual center of the whole city. In relation to the natural territorial organization of Admiralty Island, the three radials were brilliantly placed. The central location of the Admiralty Building was also eminently felicitous. The central radial divides the land mass of the island into two roughly equal areas. The individual rays of the "three prongs" are almost perpendicular to the curves described by the Moika, the canal, and the Fontanka. Similarly, the Admiralty Building divides the Neva waterfront into two roughly equal parts, Dvortsovaia Quay to the east, and Angliiskaia Quay to the west. Both quays are terminated in a very successful way, the former by the Summer Garden and the Fontanka, the latter by the Kriukov Canal and Galerni Harbor (see illustration 9).

A closer study of the general plan, however, reveals a number of discrepancies and serious deficiencies in the balance of the various parts within the overall system. These faults be-

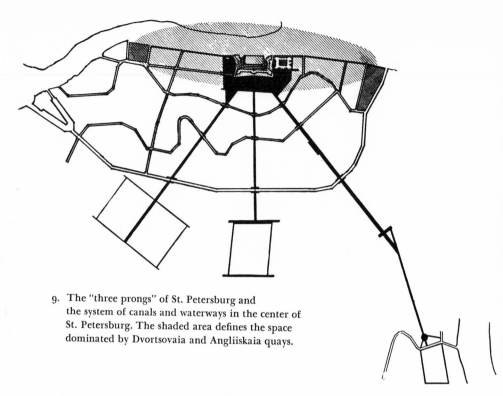

9. The "three prongs" of St. Petersburg and
the system of canals and waterways in the center of
St. Petersburg. The shaded area defines the space
dominated by Dvortsovaia and Angliiskaia quays.

come even more apparent when one attempts to analyze the
spatial relationships between the system of the "three prongs"
and the various other components of the plan, such as the
large water basin of the Neva and the layout of the other
districts of the city center (see illustration 10). Dvortsovaia
Quay together with the Summer Garden and its surrounding
areas architecturally dominate their respective counterparts
west of the central Admiralty complex. This imbalance becomes even more apparent because, in terms of their spatial
juxtaposition, the areas near the shore are not only part of
the local system of the "three prongs" but also belong to the
larger context of the whole central area of St. Petersburg.
The waters of the Neva may separate the opposite shores
physically, but they also tend to evoke their mutual spatial
and architectural relationship. Thus the radials introduce a

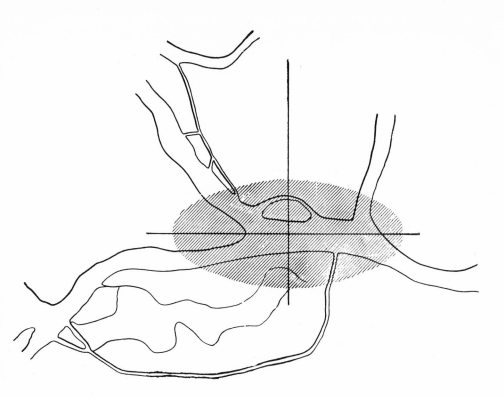

10. Top: The territory defined as the "central area of the city" (shaded), together with the so-called "natural" axes of composition. Bottom: The spatial overlap between the architectural area of influence exerted by the early city center and the newly developing system of the "three prongs" in the Admiralty District.

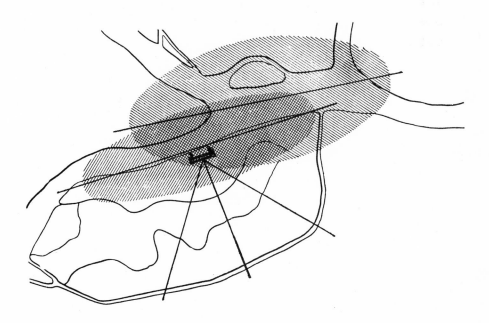

certain architectural ambiguity into the general structure of the city.

The two main districts of central St. Petersburg are separated by the waters of the Neva. The old district, founded by Peter I, represents the original ensemble of St. Petersburg. It was located near the large water basin of the Neva opposite the Peter and Paul Fortress. Due to the gradual transfer of all political and commercial activities, the center of the capital shifted to the other side of the Neva waterfront, along Nevski Prospect, and into the general area described by the other two radials. The history of the various attempts to solve these architectural and spatial contradictions is in essence the history of the planning of St. Petersburg. It is also the history of the many struggles which accompanied the attempt to resolve the dichotomy between the components of the original city and those of the later city which developed in an uncoordinated and haphazard way.

During the second half of the 18th century, the masters of Russian classicism advanced a number of highly interesting projects designed to resolve the contradictions created by the spatial imbalance of the central area of St. Petersburg. These efforts mark the second phase in the planning and design of St. Petersburg.

3

The proposed development of St. Petersburg in the second half of the 18th century

The planning projects of the second half of the 18th century represent a whole new chapter in the further development of the architectural center of St. Petersburg. They reflect a new spatial concept for the architectural organization of the central ensemble and an attempt at a more comprehensive system of planning for the whole city. Apart from being severely criticized, many of the proposed schemes were never fully realized. They were further impaired by some of the later work done in the first half of the 19th century. Nevertheless, the completed efforts of the classicists of the 18th century prepared the way for such eminent designers as Voronikhin, Zakharov, Rossi, and Thomon.

Before the official establishment of a special planning commission, a new plan for St. Petersburg was prepared and approved by the government. The commission, which was eventually appointed on December 11, 1762, was called the Commission for the Masonry Construction of St. Petersburg and Moscow. It consisted of three officials: General Chernishev, Lieutenant-General Betskov, and the wife of the Captain of the Guards, Countess Dashkov. These members were responsible for the selection of a staff of architects, surveyors, and other help as needed. The commission remained active until the year 1796. Its working staff normally consisted of one architect, one surveyor, and four to six men designated as architectural helpers.

Since the tasks faced by this commission were enormous it may be of interest to note the names of the men who worked for it at one time or another. From 1764 until his death at the end of 1772 Aleksei Vasilevich Kvasov [1] was the staff architect. He was succeeded by Ivan Egorovich Starov who also held a very important position in the Academy of Arts. The fact that he applied for the job is proof that the position of staff architect to the commission was an important one. I. Starov served for approximately two years and in 1774 transferred his duties to his colleague at the Academy, Prof. A. Ivanov.

In discussing Ivanov's character and professional abilities, V. Bazhenov wrote:

I examined with great interest and pleasure the projects presented to me by the honorable member of the St. Petersburg Academy of Arts, Alekseievich, son of Ivan. I also listened to his learned dissertation, and after doing thus, resolved, that having been sent by the Academy to Paris and

Rome for study, he, indeed, did not waste his time there. After his return he made excellent use of his acquired professional skill and knowledge and must therefore be considered as a most worthy member of the architectural profession. As a testimony of this I bestowed upon him on January 31, 1774, in the city of St. Petersburg a Certificate of Honor.[2]

Ivanov was followed by Ivan Leim, who filled the post of staff architect until the dissolution of the commission.

The work of the commission on the city of St. Petersburg was confined to the first half of its existence, i.e., the sixties and the seventies. Later it occupied itself with the planning of the various district and provincial capitals of Russia. In the history of the planning of St. Petersburg the works of A. V. Kvasov, I. E. Starov, and A. A. Ivanov (and their assistants)[3] are of great interest.

One of the first acts of the commission was its announcement, in 1763, of an international competition for the planning of St. Petersburg. This was the first time that the conditions of an open competition had been published in a newspaper and they are of great interest both because of their organization and because they spell out a detailed program for the planning of St. Petersburg. The competition rules were published on November 14, 1763, in *Supplement No. 91* of the *St. Petersburg News.* It was announced that:

> . . . the commission will be susceptible to such proposals as would bestow upon the city of St. Petersburg a state of dignity and grandeur, commensurate with its position as the capital of a large country . . . for the purpose of which it has been resolved to call upon all architects, Russian and foreign, and also including all other interested amateurs, to apply their labors to the composition of a plan for the said city of St. Petersburg, together with a written dissertation. In order to proceed in the correct manner, the following in-

structions must be followed in order to qualify: All applicants must apply for the base-plans of the city of St. Petersburg in writing. These plans depict the city in its present state. . . .

Each project was to be accompanied by two separate designs, complete with all the necessary dimensions and descriptions. In addition to the plans a written explanation had to be provided describing clearly and in detail where and how each building was to be located and giving reasons for the choice of a particular solution as well as an explanation of its special merits. In the first proposal the existing conditions of the city had to be taken into account. Built-up and important streets were to be fully respected and were not to be broken up (except when deemed absolutely necessary). They were to be improved and adjusted and their imperfections corrected. New buildings were to be placed on squares and open spaces according to need. In short, all the existing parts of the city were to be brought into mutual harmony and good order, for the greater pleasure and use of its citizens, and befitting a spacious capital city of a great empire. In the second project the designers were given complete freedom and had permission to submit whatever scheme they thought would best achieve the above goals regardless of existing conditions. In both cases an architectural definition of the central part of the city and the development of the spatial relationship between it and the suburbs—which had grown up in a random and haphazard way—was to be considered, and potential problems solved.

After the entries had been received by the commission each was identified by a letter of the alphabet and, accompanied by the written explanation, put up for general exhibition. The exhibit remained open for fifteen days from early morning till late at night. At the end of this period a jury of chosen experts—including all of the contestants—was asked to judge the entries. These experts were asked to state their order of preference and to express their views in writing. They were further asked to give their opinions on the practicability of each scheme, describing in detail which parts were capable of realization and which not. After all the schemes had been reviewed by the general jury, the commission was to weigh all the evidence and make a final decision. The commission was furthermore asked to decide which plans were to be approved; which parts of the rejected plans could possibly be realized; which schemes were superior in terms of their composition—including their feasibility; and finally, what the number and cash value of the awards should be.

If the competition material had been preserved, many interesting facts concerning the development of St. Petersburg and its individual areas would have been handed down to us. All that has been found so far is a list of the participants whose designs were accepted by the commission and actually carried out. Among these were: the Director of the Imperial Academy of Arts, A. Kokorinov, the Academician, Vallin de la Mothe; the Royal Prussian Court Architect, Georg Christopher Berger; Captain Carl Hontard, and others. One may therefore safely assume that the consequent planning of the city owed much to the designs submitted for this competition.

During the years from 1764 to 1767 the commission developed additional planning proposals for the various districts of the city. These separate schemes were later transferred to a master plan of the whole city which was ultimately submitted for approval. Many years of work by many architects went into this composite plan which was the first official attempt to view the plan of the city as a whole.

In order to understand the complexity of the problem which the masters of Russian classicism had to solve, one has

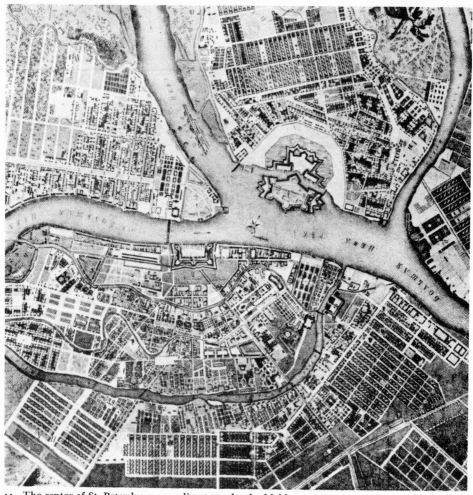

11. The center of St. Petersburg according to a plan by Makhaev, 1753.

merely to examine the fragmented plan of the city as it was
in 1753, published by the Academy of Science (see illustration 11). It shows the city consisting of three independent
parts, each separated from the other by the two main branches
of the Neva. The Admiralty District, i.e., the center of the
city, is the only sector which displays the beginning of a definite planning concept. Even here the radials are still badly
defined and hemmed in on all sides by irregular building

masses. Only in combination with the Neva, the Moika, the Fontanka, and the future Ekaterinski Canal does the structural skeleton of the city center become obvious. One can also discern the beginning of the formation of such future important streets as Kazanskaia, Sadovaia, and Galernaia.

During this period the Winter Palace, designed by Rastrelli, was being finished; the Summer Garden was being remodeled; and the steeple of the Admiralty Tower could be seen at the end of the three radials. Before its reconstruction, the modesty of the old Admiralty contrasted severely with Rastrelli's rich architectural forms, but Korobov's spire topped by a small golden ship was the same as it is today.

The planning of Vasilevski Island had already been started in Peter I's time. The island was laid out according to a regular gridiron system, quite monotonous and without any major architectural focus. The structure of the Petersburg District can be observed on the 1753 plan which illustrates the random quality of its layout and the absence of any kind of planning concept whatsoever. The fact that there were no major structures on the Petersburg side at that time explains why its replanning was considered first.[4] It is quite certain that the plan of 1753 represented a somewhat idealized version of the city, and that its actual appearance was much more disorderly than the plan indicated.

Of the three fragments, two needed visual unification most, namely the Admiralty District and Vasilevski Island opposite. The task was unusually complex, but a careful study of the various schemes advanced during that period proves that the planners of the Russian capital were highly skillful practitioners of their art. The difficult task was approached with imagination and daring. Both the Admiralty District and Vasilevski Island were left unchanged, but a new system of radials was proposed for the Petersburg District. These radials were designed to converge upon the Peter and Paul Fortress, with the spire of Peter and Paul Cathedral as their focal element (see illustration 12). The remainder of the Petersburg District was organized in a large semicircle around the Kronberg Arsenal. The design thus focused on the fortress, and past it—by means of the large masses of the fortress—on the Neva. The new radials for the Petersburg District were designed as a spatial counterpart to the emerging system of the "three prongs" on the Admiralty side. They were similar in character but different in their geometric details. Both systems were oriented toward the Neva by virtue of the radials. In both cases the radials and the spires of the focal elements were the most important architectural features of the whole design. But there the similarity ends. Whereas the waterfront along the Neva on the Admiralty side was developed along a broad front on each side of the Admiralty, all of the building masses on the opposite shore were made to converge upon the Kronberg Arsenal and the Peter and Paul Fortress (see illustration 12). The new plan for the Petersburg District may have achieved the task of balancing the two parts separated by the Neva, but it did not solve the greater problem of giving the whole city a coherent spatial structure.

The river was, as it still is, the main element dividing the various separate parts of the city. The chief problem facing the designers was the task of unifying the three main territories divided by the confluence of the two principal branches of the Neva: Vasilevski Island, the Petersburg District, and the Admiralty District. A balance among these three central areas was eventually achieved because the Admiralty District at that time already had a definite spatial structure. However, the task of unifying the various disparate elements was not solved in its entirety by proposing another set of radials. The problem of how to tie the three fragments of Vasilevski Island,

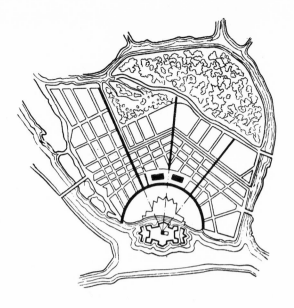

12. Top: Planning scheme for the Petersburg District.
Bottom: Planning scheme for the Admiralty District.

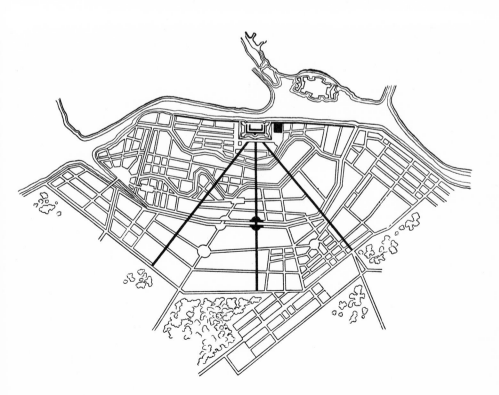

the Petersburg District, and the Admiralty District into one coherent visual whole remained as vexing as ever. The answer to this dilemma depended upon the resolution of the visual interrelationships among the three islands across the waters of the Neva.

We must now consider the nature of this node and what the designers did to find a solution for a difficult architectural problem. The main axes of the proposed two radial systems were displaced with respect to each other. This displacement was the result of the position of their two focal elements, namely the Peter and Paul Fortress on the Petersburg side and the Admiralty on the mainland side. The direction of this spatial displacement pointed toward the third fragment of the ensemble, i.e., the Strelka of Vasilevski Island. The planners were convinced that the largest and most important buildings should be located along Dvortsovaia Quay, others near the Peter and Paul Fortress, and others still on the Strelka of Vasilevski Island, thus forming the new architectural center.

There is one basic architectural contradiction inherent in this scheme: assuming that Dvortsovaia Quay, the Peter and Paul Fortress, and the Strelka of Vasilevski Island were to become the main elements in the larger structure of the city, then logically and in terms of the overall spatial equilibrium the eastern portion of the Admiralty District would have to be made architecturally much more significant. However, a closer examination of the Admiralty District as an independent element reveals that its visual center of gravity is definitely determined by the Admiralty itself. To the right and left of it extend Dvortsovaia and Angliiskaia quays, both intrinsically of equal visual importance. However, conceived as part of the total scheme, Dvortsovaia Quay certainly warranted a stronger architectural emphasis than it had received before.

Another shift of emphasis resulting from these discrepancies in the general plan was the violation of the symmetry of the "three prongs." The planning of the central radial was neglected, and Nevski Prospect, which is closest to Dvortsovaia Quay, became the dominant element in the system of the "three prongs." The proposals made by the masters of Russian classicism during the second half of the 18th century and the first half of the 19th century—to develop and build up Nevski Prospect and to strengthen its architectural relationship with respect to the other two radials—become logical and necessary only when one considers the system of the "three prongs" in the context of the larger system of the whole central ensemble. Although this violation of the symmetry of the radials was necessary, it unfortunately did not solve all the problems created by the existing fragmentation of the city into separate and unrelated areas. To achieve a unified concept other measures had to be taken.

In the planning and development of the Strelka of Vasilevski Island the complexity and imbalance of the spatial structure of the city had to be carefully considered. As a result the development of the Strelka assumed vital importance in finding the correct architectural solution to the planning problems of the whole central ensemble. The question is a complicated one and includes so many controversial elements that each problem will be taken up in turn later. For the moment it is enough to say that the inclusion of the Strelka into the general system of the central area called not only for the balancing of the whole ensemble but also for the visual "tying in" of the two spires which represented the focal points upon which the two radial systems were designed to converge.

In spite of all these efforts at achieving coherence, the plan of St. Petersburg in the middle of the 18th century in fact merely represented the sum of many unrelated fragments. The creation of a second system of radials on the Petersburg side would have made this fragmentation even more apparent, even though a considerable balance between the two main areas of the center would have been achieved. The designers hoped that an integrated main ensemble would act as a strong unifying element, tying together all the disparate fragments of the plan. In order to achieve this it was necessary to take into consideration the spatial imbalance of the general plan, which was clearly the result of the fragmentation of the various structural elements which faced the river at different angles, as well as of the architectural diversity of some of the larger complexes facing the Neva.

The general plan was approved, thus influencing the future spatial structure of the whole city. The complexity of the task was compounded by the fact that many accommodations had to be made to existing conditions. Dvortsovaia Quay and the large panorama across the river soon became the two most important architectural ensembles of St. Petersburg. The main elements of the panorama across the Neva were the Peter and Paul Fortress and the Strelka of Vasilevski Island. This huge new ensemble replaced the original city center which had previously been confined to Vasilevski Island. At that time the Strelka had only secondary significance. In view of these new conditions, the spatial and architectural importance of the harbor, the fortress, and the old city center on Vasilevski Island had to be re-evaluated. In the second half of the 18th century all these diverse functions of the city became secondary and had to be subordinated to its primary function as the center of the national government and the capital of Russia. The Imperial Palace and the buildings along Dvortsovaia Quay had by that time become the most important architectural elements in the city.

It should be noted that, even after the inclusion of the central ensemble into the system of Dvortsovaia Quay, the complex of the Admiralty still remained its most important element, mainly because it visually tied the radials of the Admiralty District to the spaces of the main ensemble.

The planners of the classical period further proposed that a number of open squares should be created within the central part of the city. These were: Senate Square, Birzhevaia Square, the Tsaritsin Luga, Dvortsovaia Square and a main square on the Petersburg side. Beyond these extended the "three prongs," penetrating the adjacent territory and connecting it to the main ensemble. Apart from their particular virtues or faults, these proposals reflected quite accurately many of the difficulties which entered into the design of the new center of the capital. The next chapter will show to what degree these plans were realized and to what extent they had to be changed in order to adapt to new and unforeseen conditions.

4

The actual development of St. Petersburg in the second half of the 18th century

The granite facing of the Neva waterfront, the stone refacing of the Peter and Paul Fortress, and the planning of Dvortsovaia Quay were the first projects to be undertaken according to the new general plan (see illustration 13). The granite facing of the Neva waterfront was started in 1764 under the supervision of Iu. Feldten.[1]

In the previous analysis of the planning project for the central area of St. Petersburg in the first half of the 18th century we mentioned the great importance of Dvortsovaia Quay in the overall system of the central ensemble. Let us now examine its functional significance in the life of the city dur-

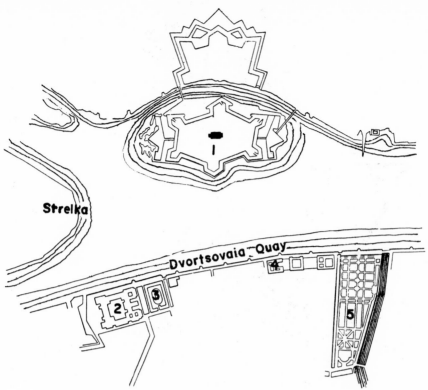

13. The most important architectural elements of the central ensemble
of St. Petersburg included in the reconstruction works during the
second half of the 18th century. 1. Peter and Paul Fortress;
2. Winter Palace; 3. Hermitage; 4. Marble Palace; 5. Summer Garden.

ing that period. Dvortsovaia Quay was the main circulation
link between the Winter Palace and the Summer Garden, at
that time the main recreational area for the aristocracy. In
fact, it may be said that Dvortsovaia Quay and all the buildings between it and Millionaia Street represented the architectural image of aristocratic St. Petersburg. Graceful coaches
and elegant carriages filled Dvortsovaia Quay, while light
galleys, flying the imperial colors, anchored opposite the Jordan entrance of the Winter Palace.

The most important task in the design of the waterfront
was the spatial juxtaposition of the buildings along the water-

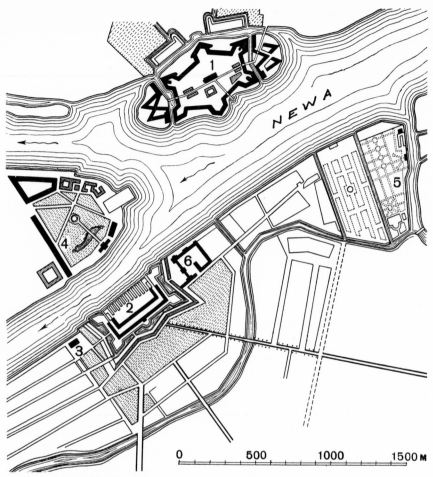

14. Central area of St. Petersburg *ca.* 1750. 1. Peter and Paul Fortress;
2. Admiralty; 3. St. Isaac Cathedral; 4. The Twelve Collegia;
5. Summer Garden; 6. Original Winter Palace.

front with the sweeping grandeur of the Neva (see illustration 14). History attests to the fact that Feldten and other
masters met the challenge with great skill and competence.
The best description of the main characteristics of the Neva
waterfront can be found in I. Grabar's *History of Russian
Art.* It reads in part:

A task of such magnitude could be taken on only by a great
artist, who would refuse to get lost in details and who would

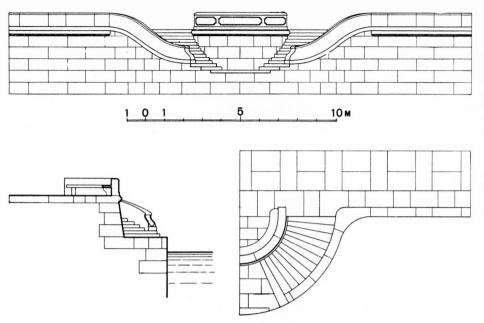

1 0 1　　　　5　　　　10 M

15. Neva quays. Steps leading to boat landing at the north end of
Senate Square.

not for one minute lose sight of the larger aesthetic goal
. . . the somber lines of this gigantic band of granite, severe
even when they descend to the Neva by steps, the finish of
the water gates and the junction with the canal inlets, all
this provided St. Petersburg with a unique and beautiful
waterfront, and became one of the most characteristic land-
marks of the city.[2]

The quays of the Neva were the foundation upon which
the main ensemble of the city was erected. The granite facing
of the waterfront predetermined to a large degree the principles for the design of its buildings, especially since all construction along the quays was situated very close to the edge
of the Neva. The most significant architectural characteristics
of the granite facing are its continuity and architectural unity.
These were achieved by the use of a single material—granite;
by a uniform slope toward the Neva; and finally, by the consistent way in which all the stonework was finished (see il-

lustration 15). In order to achieve visual and aesthetic unity between the granite quays and the buildings above, it was necessary to strive for a similar degree of monumentality, unifying the whole façade by controlling height and the general direction of the cornice lines and by the strong architectural articulation of the façades facing the Neva.

The existing buildings along Dvortsovaia Quay did not possess the qualities described above, and thus the question of their reconstruction had to be considered. In February, 1765, the Commission for Masonry Construction sent a report to Empress Catherine II (1762–96) which reads in part:

An increase in the overall height of all the buildings [along the Neva] is deemed imperative, first, to create a greater number of residences . . . and second, to bring them into harmony with the grandeur of the granite quays, which are famous all over the world for their beauty and utility.[3]

The proposal was approved and reconstruction of Dvortsovaia Quay was started from both ends—from the Winter Palace in the west and the Summer Garden in the east. The ornamental fence of the Summer Garden, the palaces of Betskov and Saltykov, the storehouse of the Marble Palace, and the Marble Palace itself made up the first imposing block, occupying almost one third of the waterfront. The Winter Palace, the Old Hermitage, the so-called Reserve Palace, and the Hermitage Theater occupied a similar area at the other end. In addition to the dramatic contrast between the buildings along the quays and the water surface of the Neva the central ensemble further enhanced the contrast of the architectural spaces facing each other across the Neva. Dvortsovaia Quay represented a unified front of adjoining monumental palaces. The panorama on the opposite side of the river consisted of the verdure around the Kronberg, the stone walls of the Peter and Paul Fortress, the tower of Peter and Paul Cathedral and the broad perspectives of the branches of the Neva.

In order to realize this concept it was necessary to give the buildings along the waterfront—from the Winter Palace to the Summer Garden—a unified architectural character. This was not only prompted by the need to create an aesthetic integration between the granite of the shorelines and the buildings above, but was also a recognition of the strong plastic forms of the Peter and Paul Fortress located on the opposite side of the Neva. Only in view of all these circumstances, and particularly because of its important central location, can one understand why Dvortsovaia Quay became such an important element in the system of the central ensemble, especially in terms of its architectural expression. The commission was aware of this, and from the beginning insisted on developing the waterfront with "a single façade."

The line of buildings between the Winter Palace and the Hermitage Theater represents a superb example of the translation of these principles into reality. The first and most successful step in the formation of this new ensemble was Vallin de la Mothe's [4] construction of the Old Hermitage, in the period 1764 to 1767, in line with the Winter Palace. The architect's main task was to create subtle architectural relationships between the elevations of the Winter Palace and those of the new project in order to achieve a unified ensemble. This presented difficulties mainly because of the stylistic differences between Rastrelli's vivid and expressive baroque and the newly emerging classicism of the 18th century. In his *History of Russian Art,* I. Grabar writes: "Vallin de la Mothe thought it necessary to repeat certain features of the Winter Palace for the sake of architectural unity." [5] Let us examine then, which elements de la Mothe used in the design of the Old Hermitage to achieve architectural unity with the Winter Palace.

Comparing the two buildings it is easy to discover their common architectural characteristics. For one, the height of both buildings is almost identical. Both are divided into two parts horizontally by intermediate cornice lines. The proportion of the base to the upper stories is also similar. In each building there are four rows of windows located at equal height and of equal size and proportions. Furthermore, the upper floors of both buildings are decorated by Corinthian columns. These are the main features common to both buildings. The Hermitage maintains a close kinship to the baroque of the Winter Palace in other ways as well, especially in the picturesque projection of its central part, in the design of the pedestals and the porticoes, and in its finish. Due to this similarity of architectural expression the Hermitage and the Winter Palace form a unified architectural ensemble without losing their individuality. Thus de la Mothe translated the theoretical principle of a "unified façade" for the Neva waterfront into architectural reality.

The design of the next building, the so-called Second Hermitage or Reserve Palace (Zapasnyi Dvorets), or, as it was then called, the "building in line with the Hermitage," was assigned to Feldten in 1771. His task was much easier, since he already had de la Mothe's example as a guide. "Like de la Mothe, who found it necessary to use certain features of the Winter Palace in his design of the Hermitage, Feldten repeated certain features of the adjacent Hermitage, such as the rustication and the height of the cornice lines." [6] However, the mere copying of this or that detail would not in itself have accomplished the architectural unification of the ensemble, even though it played its part. The total effect was accomplished by more subtle means which had been first established by de la Mothe, such as massing, articulation, and overall scale relationships.

The last building in the area of Dvortsovaia Quay, where the plan called for a "unified façade" along the waterfront, was the Hermitage Theater, built by Giacomo Quarenghi.[7] His project is a good example of a building done according to the canons of the mature classicism of the 18th century, although some traces reflecting Rastrelli's picturesque baroque can still be perceived.

This concludes the period of the "unified façade" along Dvortsovaia Quay. The buildings between the Hermitage Theater and the Marble Palace were subsequently added at various other times and do not possess the same architectural unity from the point of view of overall architectural expression and conceptual clarity. Nevertheless the "tying down" of the architectural center of the city was realized to a considerable degree by virtue of the two long blocks forming a single façade from the Summer Garden to the Marble Palace, and from the Hermitage Theater to the Winter Palace.

The new buildings along Dvortsovaia Quay established a definite architectural primacy when compared with those of Angliiskaia Quay. The latter was also reconstructed during the second half of the 18th century, but most of its buildings were free-standing and architecturally unrelated to their neighbors.

After the creation of the central ensemble, the architectural organization of the Strelka was the next project to be considered. Although the cape—namely, the Strelka—of Vasilevski Island did not maintain its position as the main compositional element of the central ensemble as planned by the masters of classicism, and despite the fact that it was now Dvortsovaia Quay which represented the architectural center of the city, the Strelka nevertheless remained of vital importance in the central ensemble's overall major and minor spatial relationships.

This introduces the question of the architectural character and the spatial significance of the Strelka in the general system of the total composition. The spatial significance of the cape of Vasilevski Island is quite obviously a function of its topographical location. The Strelka is situated at a point where the river is at its widest, before it spreads to the wide surface of the large water basin where the Bolshaia and the Malaia Neva meet. Beyond, the river separates into two almost equal branches. As a result of these natural features, the central axis of the island bisects the river and passes through the tip of the island, called the Strelka. If one were to take into account the implied orientation suggested by the features of the landscape only, the architectural organization of the cape would appear to be obvious. On the basis of the foregoing, two design variants were possible: either a clear revelation of the natural axis of symmetry, as realized by Thomas de Thomon later on, or an even building up of the area of the cape, ignoring the axis. In the latter case the mass of the buildings would help to define the contours of the shore. This was in essence accomplished in Leblond's proposal.

The next question that had to be asked was: under what conditions would it be correct to express and apply the axis of symmetry to the architectural development of the cape? If the center of the city had developed on Vasilevski Island—as had been proposed in the 18th century—then the creation of a definite axis would have been justified, but only if in addition the main compositional axis of the whole central ensemble were made to pass through the cape of the island. Leblond's project had rejected such a solution and he did not articulate the axis at the cape, mainly because the main axis of the city center did not pass through the Strelka. He understood the subtle relationships among the various elements of the design, and decided to let the buildings on the Strelka follow the natural outlines of the shore.

Since the center of the city had actually developed around the Admiralty rather than on Vasilevski Island, the need for an axial composition on the Strelka became very doubtful. The creation of an axial scheme on the cape, together with the development of a central ensemble based on an architectural balance of the two opposite shores, would have given too much emphasis to elements of secondary social and aesthetic significance. Furthermore, by stressing the natural axis of the Strelka the different character of the buildings on the two opposite shores of the Neva would have been reduced to a common level of spatial and architectural importance. This also holds for the juxtaposition of the Peter and Paul Fortress and the "unified façade" of Dvortsovaia Quay. The masters of the 18th century understood this well, and in their new proposals for the planning of St. Petersburg adhered to the general principles of Leblond's proposal. Their solution certainly did not ignore the basic characteristics of the landscape, but at the same time they recognized the spatial significance of the various separate spatial elements of the ensemble, although they failed to emphasize the increased importance of the Admiralty District.

The second important element in the architectural determination of the Strelka was the spatial and visual juxtaposition of the various complexes on the opposite shores of the Neva. In Leblond's scheme the cape was developed without much regard for the architectural treatment of the opposite shores. This was only possible because in his proposal he gave social and architectural equality to both the Admiralty District and the Petersburg District opposite, treating them as subsidiary elements in relation to Vasilevski Island, which at that time represented the central area of St. Petersburg. But in time the center of the city—and with it the architectural center as well—shifted from the island across the Neva to the Admiralty District. In view of these new conditions it would have been better to strengthen the architectural expression of that part of Vasilevski Island which was located directly opposite Dvortsovaia Quay.

The functional significance of the two branches of the Neva was another important factor to be considered in the architectural organization of the Strelka. Leblond's project proposed the dredging and deepening of the Malaia Neva. In that case both branches would have become navigable and, as a result, both sides of the Strelka would have been of equal architectural importance. In view of this Leblond's architectural treatment of the cape was correct. However, Leblond's scheme was relegated to the archives, and the Bolshaia Neva, which has a deeper draught, became the main channel of navigation for seagoing vessels. Thus the side facing the navigation channel of the Bolshaia Neva become more important both functionally and aesthetically.

The actual existing layout of St. Petersburg naturally exerted considerable influence on the architectural organization of the Strelka. The street grids of the various islands around the basin of the Neva entered the plan as so many fragments, completely unrelated to each other and with each pointing at the Neva from a different direction at a different angle. Not a single unifying axis existed within the whole system, with the exception of the two local axes of the Admiralty District and the Petersburg District. The main axis of the third major quarter of the city (Vasilevski Island) was Bolshoi Prospect. It was related neither to the other two systems nor to the wide basin of the Neva. As a result the spatial

structure of the central complex became quite intricate and—
by accident—picturesque. One may therefore legitimately ask
whether there was any need to articulate the "natural" axis of
the Strelka, which would have made it even more difficult to
achieve a spatial and architectural unification of the separate
elements of the plan, especially since the more important complexes, such as the Dvortsovaia waterfront, the fortress, and
the Admiralty were already interconnected by a very complex
architectural and spatial relationship.

Such was the complicated nature of the problem which confronted the masters of the 18th century until it was brilliantly
resolved by Thomas de Thomon.[8] Assuming that the creation
of an architectural axis through the Strelka was not an absolute necessity, and assuming further that the natural outline
of the shorelines would consequently become the major de-
terminant for the proper architectural development of this
area, one comes to the inevitable conclusion that the opposite
shores facing the cape as well as the island must be regarded
as an integral part of a comprehensive architectural treatment
of the whole central area.

Three of the projects for the planning of the Strelka of
Vasilevski Island prepared by the 18th century classicists were
preserved in the archives of St. Petersburg. Each of these in
one way or another recognized the conditions discussed
above.[9]

After the Kunstkammer (housing the Museum and the
Library of the Academy of Sciences) was destroyed by fire in
the seventies it was decided to replan the area of the Strelka.
The following buildings were to be located there: the Academy of Sciences, the Academy of Arts, the University, the
Kunstkammer, the Library, the Observatory, and the Institute
of Geography (see illustration 16). The unknown author of
this design proposed to unify all these buildings into one

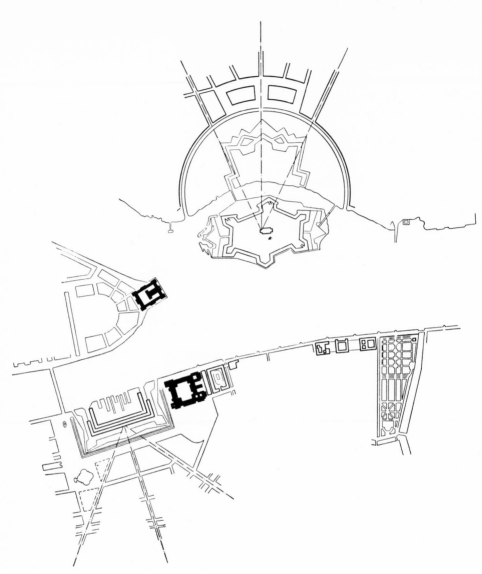

16. Planning proposal for the Strelka of Vasilevski Island in the second
half of the 18th century. This project includes the Mint and the
buildings surrounding the square in front of the Collegia.

single complex, oriented toward the Winter Palace and Dvortsovaia Quay.

The second project, also not realized, proposed to locate the Mint on the tip of the Strelka of Vasilevski Island (see illustration 17). Much as in the previous project, the axis of the Mint did not coincide with the natural axis of the island, but in this case was pointed at the Peter and Paul Fortress. The building was projected into the river toward Angliiskaia Quay, thus emphasizing the greater importance of the main branch of the Neva.

In the year 1782, Giacomo Quarenghi took over the planning of the Strelka. Apparently he used the existing official plan for St. Petersburg as the basis for his design and therefore did not change the general layout of the Strelka in a radical way. He proposed to place a major architectural element at the tip of the island, which would define the Strelka and underline its architectural significance among the neutral mass of the surrounding buildings. This major element was to be the Exchange Building (see illustration 18).

With the design of the Exchange Quarenghi achieved in one bold stroke the balance of all the other elements of the central ensemble. The slight inclination of the axis of the building from the axis of the island toward the southeast provided additional emphasis to the left bank of the Neva. The main façade of the Exchange could be seen from the full length of Dvortsovaia Quay, stretching from the Summer Garden to the Marble Palace, thus underlining the spatial importance of the mainland waterfront as a major element of the central ensemble (see illustration 16). The best view of the Exchange could be obtained from the Jordan entrance of the Winter Palace.

Contemporary critics had the following to say about Quarenghi's solution:

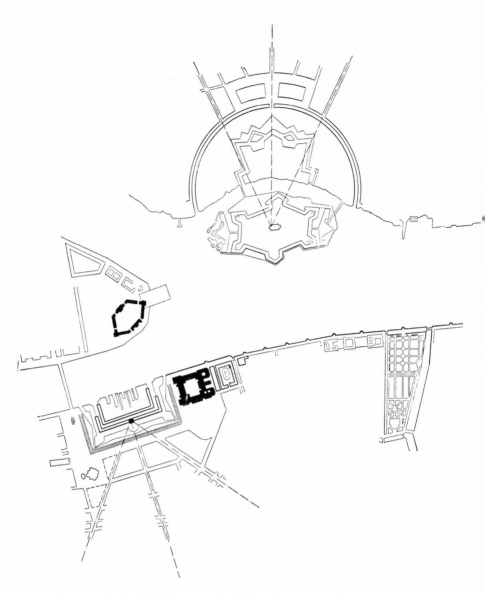

17. Planning proposal for the Strelka of Vasilevski Island in the second
half of the 18th century. The project includes the complex of the
Academy of Sciences, the Academy of Arts, the University, the Library,
the Kunstkammer, the Observatory, and the Geographical Institute.

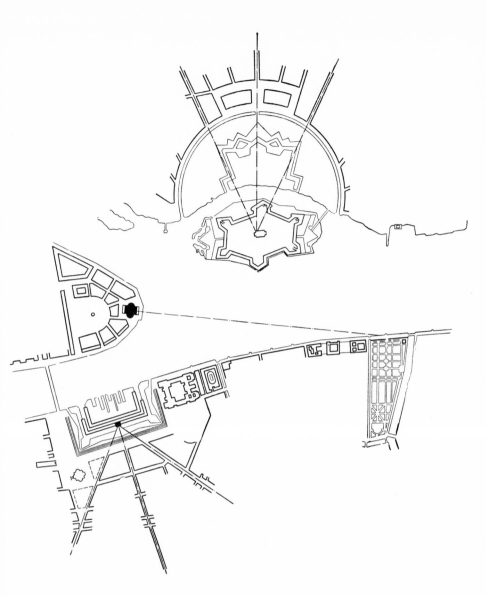

18. Planning proposal for the Strelka of Vasilevski Island in the second
half of the 18th century, showing the Exchange by Quarenghi
and the square in front of the Collegia planned by the Commission
for Masonry Construction.

At the cape of Vasilevski Island the Neva forms a large basin of water, while the two almost equal river branches introduce an element of natural symmetry. At the same time the upstream portion between the fortress and Dvortsovaia Quay forms a straight and distant view along the main body of the Neva. The natural axis is thus a result of the junction of the straight upper river and the river fork at the cape. . . . Quarenghi did not realize the extent and complexity of the design task. He was obviously faced not only with the problem of designing the Exchange on the Strelka of Vasilevski Island, but also with the problem of relating it to the whole surrounding ensemble. Seen in this context any building located at the tip of the Strelka acquires additional architectural importance precisely because of this spatial juxtaposition. However, Quarenghi restricted himself to a partial solution. By placing the Exchange at an arbitrary angle to the natural compositional axis of the island, and by giving it its own transverse axis, Quarenghi created a serious architectural contradiction with the other elements of the central ensemble.[10]

This would imply that the main axis of the Exchange should have fully coincided with the natural axis of the island. However, one can equally well assume that the orientation of the Exchange should have been subordinated to the principal elements of the ensemble and the general structure of the city center, and that the natural axis should have been treated as a secondary element only.

The same critics also assert that Quarenghi did not understand the nature of the problem within the context of the total ensemble or that he simply ignored it. This is difficult to believe, since the same Quarenghi had completed the ensemble of Dvortsovaia Quay by his design of the Hermitage Theater. Surely a great designer like Quarenghi must have been aware of such an obvious natural axis. Later critics failed to comprehend the spatial complexity of the plan into which the building had to be placed, taking as their point of departure only a single one of the many elements which determined the formation of the ensemble, thereby arriving at an incorrect interpretation of Quarenghi's extremely sensitive and truly masterful solution.

This leads to another point. In order to appreciate the value of Quarenghi's contribution, one must analyze his design according to the principles underlying 18th century planning theory. Contemporary critics make the mistake of judging the design on the basis of the planning theories of the first half of the 19th century, comparing the situation of the unfinished Exchange with Thomas de Thomon's solution.

Although not diametrically opposed, there are certain differences between the approach to the solution of spatial and architectural relationships within an ensemble characteristic of the 18th century on the one hand and of late 19th century classicism on the other. However, if an analysis is to be made at all, it must be based on the realities of a particular situation and must include an understanding of the artistic tastes and preferences of the period in question. The judgment of contemporary critics is all too often based on current opinions and ignores the historical context and ideological background which are at the root of each design philosophy. Apart from the above criteria the erroneous appraisal of the scheme is also the result of a faulty critical method. Once the building is criticized outside the context of the overall general plan which reflects the development of St. Petersburg by fragmented and unrelated spatial systems, the solution remains forever incomprehensible and irrational.

To judge Quarenghi's solution on the basis of its failure to subordinate the siting of the building to the direction of the natural axis of the landscape is to declare this axis the eternal and unchangeable measure of all aesthetic evaluation.

In judging Quarenghi's design as a separate element, divorced from the overall context of the central ensemble—which found its architectural expression in the confirmed planning project of St. Petersburg—and divorced as well from the actual architectural conditions of the central area, these critics clearly did not understand his aims and apparently used as their sole yardstick the solution proposed later by Thomas de Thomon, which was quite obviously based on altogether different architectural principles. Any valid analysis must consider things "and their intellectual interpretation as a function of their mutual relationships, must consider the various elements of integration, and take account of their conception and subsequent disappearance." [11]

Quarenghi's solution, as well as the solutions proposed by other 18th century planners confirm the author's opinion that the planning and design of the central area of St. Petersburg was based upon the then accepted planning project of the whole city, and that all the architects of that period acknowledged as the central issue of all their many design efforts the creation of a unified central ensemble. The various city planning projects conceived in the second half of the 18th century can be appraised solely in relation to the general spatial structure of the city. The various solutions for the Strelka of Vasilevski Island are in fact a direct response to the failure of the overall concept to combine into a coherent and unified whole.

Historical documents tell the following story about the history of Quarenghi's Exchange (see illustration 19):

> The construction of a stone Exchange Building, located on Vasilevski Island, near the Imperial Academy of Sciences, proceeded in the following manner: (a) 16 October 1782—the foundations; (b) 27 May 1784—the base; (c) 25 June 1786—16-½ arshins [12] of wall erected on top of the base.

19. G. Quarenghi. The Exchange of St. Petersburg, main façade.

In a communication concerning budgetary matters dated January 29, 1787, there is a copy of a letter which contained a directive from Her Imperial Majesty. This ordered the suspension of all monetary allocation for the year 1787 for the construction of the St. Petersburg Exchange and indicated that what should be done was "to cover it with . . . a temporary roof only." On February 25, 1787, the architect G. Quarenghi dispatched a report in which he wrote that "the construction is well covered." In 1788, in another report, Quarenghi explained that the temporary roof should be carefully inspected "to protect the walls from moisture and decay." [13] In 1789 additional sums of money were released for the continuation of the construction. Quarenghi reported that: "the two external staircases of the Exchange should be covered by a temporary roof before the onset of freezing weather, since the mortar has not yet set. . . ." [14]

Funds for the building were cut off again in the following

year, but this was not due to any specific discontent concerning the project or the activities of the architect. Documents reveal that the building was beset with constant misfortune. In 1793 the construction watchman reported that: "On June 7, a storm tore off the wooden roof entirely and damaged the iron work of the Exchange Building located here on Vasilevski Island. . . ." and that "the scaffoldings have collapsed." [15] An estimate of the most urgent repairs was requested and the money was later duly released.

However, the unfinished building continued to deteriorate, and after the death of Catherine II work on it was stopped altogether. Tsar Paul, who disliked all works undertaken by his predecessor, ordered the Exchange to be transferred from governmental care to the jurisdiction of the Justice Department. A few years later a commission was appointed to determine the fate of the Exchange, and it was eventually decided that it was not practical to continue with its construction. This episode brought to a close the work begun in the 18th century to create the central ensemble around the large water basin of the Neva.

The second cycle of reconstruction works within the central area of the city was the subsequent planning and development of the terminal node of the Admiralty radials (see illustration 20). We mentioned earlier that the "three prongs" of the Admiralty District were the most important element in the system of the central ensemble of St. Petersburg. The architectural integration of this system with the main ensemble of the city was therefore of primary importance. Without such an integration the system would have remained isolated from the other significant spatial and structural elements of the Admiralty District. An engraving by Makhaev and Atkinson's panorama illustrate the condition of this

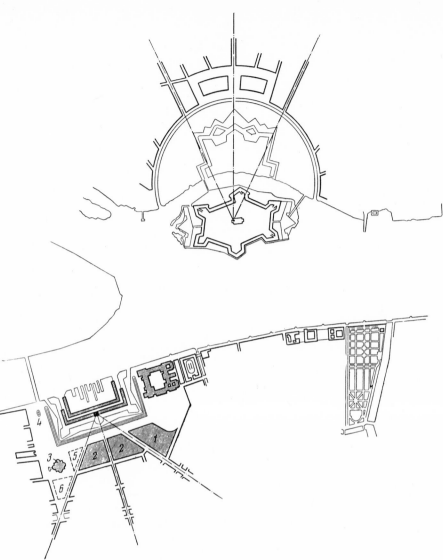

20. Schematic plan showing the main architectural elements of the
Admiralty District in the second half of the 18th century. 1–2.
Existing buildings; 3. St. Isaac Cathedral; 4. Equestrian statue of
Peter I; 5–6. Undeveloped lots.

node before the beginning of the reconstruction works in the second half of the 18th century.

In order to integrate the radials with the system of the main ensemble it was first of all necessary to organize the space around the Admiralty in an architectural manner, attempting its organic integration with the line of buildings along Dvortsovaia Quay. In 1765 a plan was approved proposing the development for residential purposes of most of the open space in front of the Admiralty. According to this plan various residential buildings were erected opposite the Winter Palace and two others opposite the Admiralty itself. These buildings defined the limits of two of the future central squares, namely Dvortsovaia Square and Admiralty Square. Apart from terminating the main portion of the "unified front" which had its beginning at the Summer Garden, Senate Square was equally important architecturally for the creation of the central ensemble and its spatial integration with the "three prongs" of the Admiralty District.

In order to achieve an integration of the various fragments within the Admiralty District, the old St. Isaac Church —located between the Admiralty Building and the Senate Building in line with buildings along Angliiskaia Quay—had to be demolished. The removal of the church opened the square toward the Neva. This open space confronting the river was similar to another one near the Summer Garden and Isaakovski Bridge. The third St. Isaac Cathedral, which was built according to the design of Antonio Rinaldi [16] in the rear part of Senate Square, became the final important component of the central ensemble, mainly because of its special location. While the cathedral was being erected in the depth of the square, the equestrian statue of Peter I was being put up near the edge of the Neva.

The placing of the statue was not determined upon at

once.[17] The statue—which had achieved considerable fame long before its completion—was considered to be of great political importance by Catherine II and her court. Obviously, the Bronze Horseman deserved to be placed in the most important part of the city center. Its location in Senate Square demonstrates beyond any doubt that the left bank of the Neva between the Summer Garden and the Senate Building was considered the most important area of the city as well as the main element of the central ensemble in the second half of the 18th century.

The residential development in front of the Admiralty, the construction of St. Isaac Cathedral, the continuous line of buildings along Dvortsovaia Quay, and the erection of the monument to Peter I were of utmost importance for the proper architectural development and the spatial definition of the city center. However, even more important was the proposed reconstruction of the Admiralty itself. The main reason for this is the central location of the building within the Admiralty District and the spatial importance of the tower which, as it were, held the "three prongs" together at their point of convergence. The documents which have been found, prove that this task was understood by the planners, and that the reconstruction of the Admiralty was a direct result of these considerations. It was furthermore proposed to transfer the Admiralty staff to Kronstadt and to house the Senate in its place.

In 1783 a fire broke out in the old Admiralty, and shortly after the conflagration the following ukase was issued:

. . . we find it opportune and in accordance with necessary improvements to move the Admiralty from our capital to Kronstadt . . . we also propose that the building, now occupied by the Admiralty, and located in our capital, be converted to another use, which is in full accordance with a decision reached by the collegia; thus only the most urgent repairs should be undertaken, in view of the fact that the said building may be used for its present purpose for a short period of time only.[18]

However, members of the Admiralty staff were very reluctant to move out of the capital to Kronstadt. They did not dare to contravene the imperial order directly, but instead they presented the government with an exceedingly high estimate for the cost of moving and the construction of a new edifice in the new location. This maneuver achieved its purpose, and the Admiralty was not rebuilt in the 18th century. Because of this delay the last architectural link between the central ensemble along the Neva waterfront and the "three prongs" of the Admiralty District was left unfinished.

At this point it seems appropriate to review the principal significant factors in the formation of the central ensemble of St. Petersburg during the second half of the 18th century. The two main considerations during the founding period of St. Petersburg in Peter I's time were: the selection of a suitable territory and the siting of important buildings, such as the fortress and the port structures. These buildings were a direct response to the primary functional needs of their time, namely defense and trade. After the transfer of the capital from Moscow to St. Petersburg, the actual paper planning for the capital city was begun as best exemplified in the plan proposed by Leblond. His project recognized the political, social, and aesthetic needs of that period and gave them architectural expression. It achieved the formal integration of the design with the natural features of the river delta, and ultimately combined into one plan the best features of city planning as practiced in France and the Scandinavian countries during that period. Unfortunately the project could not be realized, as it was beyond the technical and financial capabilities of Russia at that time. As a result the growing capital had no coherent master plan and developed instead according to local planning efforts centering around the Peter and Paul Fortress and the Admiralty. These two complexes became the architectural foci of the city center concurrently with the creation of the "three prongs," and, in combination with the transfer of the political life of the city from Vasilevski Island to the Admiralty District, this made the Admiralty the most significant architectural element within the spatial structure of the central area of the city. The natural features around the Admiralty were poor compared with the dramatic location of the Peter and Paul Fortress. This created a contradiction in terms of visual balance between the natural features of the Petersburg District and the formal, man-made elements of the Admiralty District. The plan of the central part of the city was therefore very poorly balanced.

The various planning proposals which were advanced by the masters of Russian classicism during the second half of the 18th century made serious attempts to achieve a spatial and architectural balance among the disparate fragments of the overall plan. This proved to be an extremely difficult task. The solutions are interesting in that they demonstrate how difficult it was to correct the many inconsistencies caused by the uncontrolled development and random growth which had taken place during the first decades of the capital's existence. The 18th century planners tried to resolve these contradictions by developing the waterfront of the Neva in a consistent manner, thus unifying the fragments surrounding this area into one artistic whole.

It should be pointed out that two important planning ideas of the second half of the 18th century could not be realized. The first was the proposed replanning of the Petersburg side, with the resulting imbalance of the two opposite systems across the breadth of the Neva. The second was the failure to complete the composition of the central area around the Admiralty. The old Admiralty was left unchanged, while the Exchange on the Strelka of Vasilevski Island was left to fall into decay. In connection with this, one must take into consideration the magnitude of the undertaking, the enormous size of the ensemble which stretched all the way from the Senate to the Summer Garden, and also the great complexity of all the resulting spatial and architectural interrelationships. Not only was the size of the ensemble unusually big for its time, but additional time was also required to resolve the complexity of its spatial fabric. All this called for rigorous architectural discipline and great artistic skill. By adding building to building and project to project men like Vallin de la Mothe, Feldten, Quarenghi, and many others gradually created the vast ensemble in the center of St. Petersburg which is without parallel in the history of city planning. The achievement of thirty-five years of tremendous effort was impressive. What remained to be done was the reconstruction of the Admiralty, the completion of the work on the Strelka of Vasilevski Island, the replanning of the central area of the Petersburg District, and the "filling in" of the rest of the central area with excellent buildings which would be architecturally related to each other. This would raise the overall architectural quality to a higher level of expression and create a spatially unified central ensemble for the city, welding into one visual whole the unrelated fragments of the three separate islands. At the end of the 18th century all this was yet to be accomplished.

The 19th century ushered in a new era. Politically the stage was set by such major historical events as the French Revolution and the Napoleonic wars. New developments in Russia created new conditions in the political and social life of the capital, which in turn found concrete expression in new large civic works. In the process of their realization some of the projects of the 18th century were accepted while others were revised or modified, and some had to be rejected altogether because they did not respond to the changed needs of the new century.

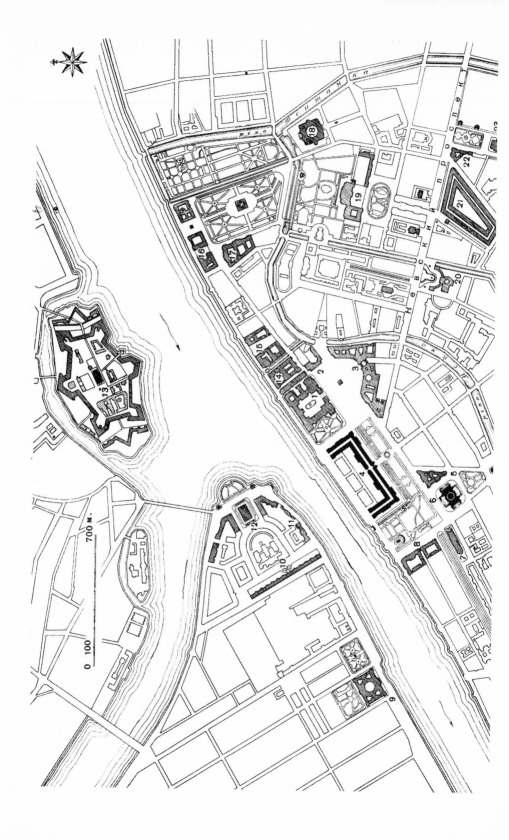

Part II

THE ENSEMBLE OF THE CENTRAL AREA OF ST. PETERSBURG IN THE 19th CENTURY

In the following chapters the "ensemble of the central area of St. Petersburg" is defined as the area covered by the system of the large central squares surrounding the Admiralty. These were: Dvortsovaia Ploshchad (Palace Square); Admiralteiskaia Ploshchad (Admiralty Square); Senatskaia Ploshchad (Senate Square); Isaakovskaia Ploshchad (St. Isaac Square); and Razvodnaia Ploshchad (Razvodnaia Square).

The architectural elements of the 18th century which were incorporated into the projects undertaken in the 19th century were: the Winter Palace designed by Rastrelli; Falconet's monument of Peter I; Korobov's Admiralty Tower; the Riding Academy of the Royal Guards by Quarenghi; and a number of old residential buildings round the Admiralty (see illustration 21).

The central ensemble—and thus the system of the five central squares—was the work of: Adrian Zakharov; Carlo di Giovanni Rossi; August Ricard (Count of Montferrand); and numerous other artists and sculptors of that period. The ensemble of the five central squares of St. Petersburg is the largest, most complex, and at the same time the most interesting architectural ensemble created in Russia in the first half of the 19th century.

21. Central area of St. Petersburg. 1. Winter Palace; 2. Staff Building of the Royal Guards Regiments; 3. General Staff Building; 4. Admiralty; 5. House of Lobanov-Rostovski; 6. St. Isaac Cathedral; 7. Royal Guards Riding Academy; 8. Senate and Synod; 9. Academy of Arts; 10. The Twelve Collegia; 11. Academy of Sciences and Kunstkammer; 12. The Exchange; 13. Peter and Paul Fortress; 14. The Hermitage; 15. The Hermitage Theater; 16. Marble Palace; 17. Barracks of Paul's Regiment; 18. Mikhailovski Castle; 19. Mikhailovski Palace; 20. St. Kazan Cathedral; 21. Gostinyi Dvor; 22. Library; 23. Alexander Theater.

5

The center of St. Petersburg in the 19th century

The 18th century left a mixed legacy to the planners of the 19th century. The architects of the 18th century must be credited with the general plan for St. Petersburg, the building of the granite retaining walls along the Neva waterfront, the rebuilding of Dvortsovaia Quay, and the development of Nevski Prospect. These works were carried out over a period of more than thirty years, and many of them remained unfinished. The rapidly changing character of the city and the new social conditions came into conflict with the old planning methods. The old concepts of spatial organization proved inadequate to the needs of the new century.

In order to comprehend the subsequent architectural development of St. Petersburg, a short glance back may be in order. We left the Strelka of Vasilevski Island at a time when the construction of Quarenghi's Exchange had been discontinued and the building was gradually deteriorating. The central issues in the planning of the architectural center of St. Petersburg are the key to a proper understanding of the aesthetic and ideological changes which coincided with the accession to the throne of Alexander I. These changes found their architectural expression in the stylistic character and designs of the Russian classicism of the first half of the 19th century.

The masters of 18th century classicism attached the greatest importance to the following two principles of city design. The first was the conviction that "no effort should be spared to make the city more beautiful and more magnificent," and that "nothing serves this purpose better than to fill the central area with significant buildings and regular squares." [1] The second principle resulted in the creation of a system in which "all the buildings of the ensemble would follow one overall general line with all the building façades arranged in such a way as to form a continuous front, without projecting porticoes, and of equal height." [2]

The most beautiful and most successful example of both these principles is the line of buildings along Dvortsovaia Quay between the Winter Palace and the Hermitage Theater. The general character of these buildings is in full harmony with the spatial character of the waterfront. Each building retains its individual features, and an integrated frontal composition is achieved by controlling the general height, the alignment of the cornice lines, and other unifying architectural devices.

However, the experience of carrying out such vast projects

in the center of the city during the second half of the 18th century had proved that such schemes were difficult to realize. To fill the central area of the city with "monumental buildings" and to build all streets "from one intersection to the next with one unified, continuous façade" was impossible, except under special circumstances. Gradually the whole principle had to be discarded for the simple reason that it was beyond the technical and financial capabilities of the current art of city building. This is proved by the fact that even in the very heart of the central ensemble—along Dvortsovaia Quay—the principle of the "continuous façade" was incapable of full realization. Obviously, it would have been even more difficult in the other quarters of the city. The square at the intersection of the Fontanka and Gorokhovia Street may serve as a good example.

The square is located in front of the bridge over the Fontanka and was created in the second half of the 18th century. Its planning can be considered typical of all "residential development" during that period. A copy of the general plan of the Admiralty District which also included the plan of the square, together with a drawing of its "general elevations," was sent by the Commission for Masonry Construction to police headquarters, which employed an architect on its staff. He was supposed to ensure that all construction would be carried out as indicated on the plan. According to this plan the square was to be surrounded by a semicircular row of buildings, all unified by a continuous main façade of equal height. However, most of the lots around the square eventually had to be subdivided and sold to different owners, since no developer could be found with enough capital to finance such a large project. As a result the square was surrounded by a number of individual buildings of different heights which were architecturally unrelated to each other. Another conflict between reality and planning theory stemmed from the impossibility of creating a long continuous façade without rigid control of the actual construction sequence. The practical implementation of the concept of a "unified façade" was possible only under exceptional conditions where the individual buildings could be erected one after the other in a predetermined sequence. This was done along part of Dvortsovaia Quay, and in some other special cases of simultaneous development.

It should be mentioned that the Commission for Masonry Construction was well aware of these difficulties. At one point a proposal was advanced suggesting that in important areas of the city, and around squares, the front walls of the buildings be erected at "government expense," leaving it to the owners to add their own buildings at the rear. This proposal, however, was never put into practice. Such, then, were the gradually emerging contradictions between paper planning and actual building practices.

Another reason for the uneven development of St. Petersburg was the desire of the ruling classes to first of all create a prestige center for the capital at the expense of the other parts of the city. The practical failure of the first comprehensive planning project for St. Petersburg which had been proposed by the Commission for Masonry Construction in the first half of the 18th century revealed the discrepancy between theoretical concept and actual building practice. The new needs of a new era required a different architectural organization of space.

Since the old methods of city planning had failed in terms of their universal application, new principles of spatial organization had to be formulated which would satisfy the political, social, and architectural requirements of the new century. Before attempting any new solution it had to be acknowledged that it was impossible to "fill" the entire city or even the large central ensemble with "monumental edifices" architecturally "tied" one to the other. This led to the obvious conclusion that a more economical and effective distribution of a limited number of monumental buildings would present a better solution. Due to their large size and civic importance these were usually built and financed either by government departments or by rich and influential members of the court.

In order to replace the continuous line of mutually interconnected buildings by a limited number of free-standing monumental structures the latter had to be carefully situated in the most important locations within the spatial structure of the city. In terms of their architectural significance, these key elements had to replace the former notion of the "unified front." Looked at through the extensive perspectives of the straight avenues and along the quays, these monumental edifices were intended to connect the large spaces of the city visually by switching the view from one important space to the next, thus making the relative imperfections of the intermediate "gray areas" less noticeable. These intermediate secondary spaces could then be filled with buildings of lesser importance.

The two most important elements entering the spatial structure of the center of St. Petersburg were the Neva quays and the system of the "three prongs." With this in mind it was not too difficult to determine the locations in which key buildings should be placed first. In the river area it was the Strelka of Vasilevski Island which closed the grand perspective of the large water surface of the river basin at the place where the three islands came together. This was also the spot where the Gornyi Institute—which terminated the view along the main river channel of the Bolshaia Neva—was finally built. In the system of the "three prongs" the focal point of the radial system was defined by the tower of the old Admiralty. It is therefore no accident that at the beginning of the 19th century it was decided to initiate reconstruction work concurrently in these three locations. In 1805 the construction of the new Exchange was started, and by the following year the building of the Gornyi Institute and the reconstruction of the Admiralty were under way.

In order to achieve order and organization in the vast spaces of the central area by the introduction of single monumental complexes it was necessary that these possess the following qualities: first, that they dominate the surrounding building masses; second, that they be free-standing and complete in architectural conception. The latter can be illustrated by the following example: let us imagine that we are looking from Nevski Prospect toward the tower of the Admiralty, and let us assume that the tower is only a physical protrusion in the overall façade rather than a complete architectural statement in itself. The view would then reveal only a fragment of the Admiralty with its other parts cut off by the ends of the perspectives formed by the frontal façades of Nevski Prospect. This was well understood by the designer of the tower, Adrian Zakharov.[3] In order to achieve the best effect, he designed the tower as part of the Admiralty complex only in the sense of its physical connection with the main body, but otherwise visually independent, indeed, as a clearly articulated, individual, architectural element.

The creation of dominants, and their juxtaposition with the unified façades of the existing buildings, could be achieved in several ways. It could be done by placing the monumental buildings in the most important spaces of the ensemble, or by the architectural formalization of these spaces, or by doing both. This, among other things, was reflected in a re-evaluation of the hitherto accepted aesthetic and ideological views on style. In the beginning of the 19th century I. Grabar rationalized the change as follows:

> The new age ushered in new ideas and new tasks. However, enthusiasm for the antique had not diminished in the least. On the contrary it was on the increase, and classicism flowered as never before. Still, the classicism of the 19th century was an altogether different and without any doubt a new art. It had only one thing in common with the classicism of the 18th century, namely its great admiration for the antique. Nevertheless, despite their common idealization of antiquity, there existed stylistic and formal differences between the two centuries. In the second half of the 18th century the ideal was Rome, whereas in the first half of the 19th century it was Greece.[4]

In looking for classical precedents, the new generation of designers searched amidst the ruins of Greek temples for,

> . . . new and altogether unusual forms. Even the temple of Poseidon in Paestum was considered too 'flat' and 'simple,' mainly because of its crisp lines and its severe columns. . . . It was not archaic enough for their taste, and most of them preferred the earlier temples of the 6th century, among them the so-called 'basilica' and the 'six-columned' temple of Paestum. The gigantic flat capitals of the Doric columns, their short, massive shafts tapered at the top—all of these elements were repeated in many combinations and variations in the architecture of the new century.[5]

The new principles of architectural style and spatial organization were already evident in the designs of some of the more important buildings by Voronikhin, such as the Kazan Cathedral and the Gornyi Institute, and, at its most expressive, in the Admiralty of A. Zakharov and the Exchange of Thomas de Thomon.

The new Exchange designed by Thomas de Thomon was started in 1805. It was a heavy blow to the aesthetic canons

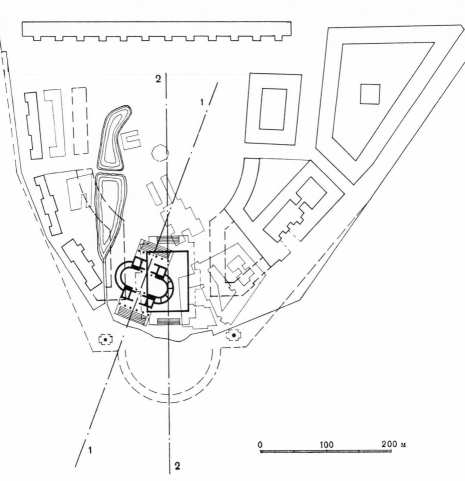

22. Strelka of Vasilevski Island showing the superimposed plans of
Quarenghi's Exchange (axis 1-1), and the new Exchange by
Thomas de Thomon (axis 2-2).

of the 18th century (see illustration 22). Even though Quarenghi's Exchange occupied the most important location
within the picturesque space of the main ensemble, it was
nevertheless—as described in detail in the previous chapter
—subordinated to its principal architectural element, namely,
the Dvortsovaia waterfront. This was in full accord with the
planning principles of the 18th century. The main purpose

for the development of the Strelka was the creation of a visual link between the Admiralty and the fortress and subsequently the whole Petersburg District. Clearly Quarenghi's Exchange took its place as one of many buildings among a row of others, and the full subtlety of the design would only have become apparent if the general plan had been carried out. Insofar as the plan was not realized, Quarenghi's siting and the architectural form of the old Exchange were severely criticized. It was finally replaced by the new Exchange designed by Thomas de Thomon.

The new project by de Thomon succeeded in completing the ensemble around the Neva basin in a single bold stroke. In architectural terms the problem was solved by a single new building and by reshaping the cape of Vasilevski Island. The organization of the Strelka was achieved by two means. First, de Thomon placed the Exchange on the natural axis of the water basin, thus subordinating all the other elements of the ensemble to the formal and spatial importance of the Strelka and making the relative imperfection of the Dvortsovaia waterfront less apparent. Second, architectural monumentality was used to reinforce the spatial importance of the building. Both these devices would have been considered quite unusual in the 18th century. By making the Exchange visually important, Thomas de Thomon directed the view away from Dvortsovaia Quay, guiding the eye in the direction of the Strelka.

By aligning the Exchange with the natural axis of the basin, and by introducing architectural monumentality, de Thomon managed to radically alter the architectural balance of all the constituent parts of the central ensemble. Main elements suddenly became secondary, and secondary ones primary. In this manner Thomon not only completed the main ensemble but also changed the architectural development of the central region of St. Petersburg, which had up to now been incomplete.

The result of this change was the architectural regrouping of the various spatial elements of the central area which the masters of the 18th century had tried to unify. The design of the Exchange complex as a complete and independent architectural group accomplished the balancing of the riparian ensemble consisting of the Strelka of Vasilevski Island on one side of the Neva and the Dvortsovaia waterfront on the other. It provided the spatial definition to the third ensemble, namely, the system of the "three prongs" near the Admiralty. The new Exchange on the Strelka marked the beginning of a new phase in the architectural development of the central area of St. Petersburg.

In the 18th century there were no functional requirements which would have called for the creation of large squares or the development of a strong spatial organization in the center of St. Petersburg. This was one of the main reasons for the failure of the plan proposed by the Commission for Stone Construction. The documents which accompanied the plans when they were submitted "for highest approval" confirm this point. In these the commission proposed "to surround the squares by beautiful buildings," and "following the example of other European cities these [open spaces] would serve the beautification of the city and in time could be filled with monuments, commemorating great Russian deeds. . . ." However, at that time the city had no need for large squares, and the plan was only partially realized. Thus the attempt to create a system of squares designed solely for the beautification of the city did not meet with great success in the 18th century.

Around 1802 the whole governmental structure of the Russian Empire was in the process of reorganization. An extensive number of ministries was set up to replace the Collegia of Peter I. These new ministries were modeled on West European governmental establishments of similar political character. This reorganization in turn called for a great number of buildings to house the new ministries. It was also one of the factors responsible for the reconstruction of the residential area opposite the Winter Palace.

The timing of the reconstruction works in the center of St. Petersburg in the 19th century coincides with a stormy period in Russian history. It was the time of Napoleon's invasion and his subsequent defeat, and a period of great military achievements by the Russian armies. St. Petersburg had always had the character of an aristocratic, military capital—Tsar Paul I having converted Tsaritsin Field into a drill ground where he conducted his continuous parades, drills, and inspections— but in the second half of the 18th century the social life of St. Petersburg had not required large squares and well developed open spaces. Now the situation had changed.

After the collapse of Napoleon's army Russian influence in European politics increased enormously and in order to maintain her position as an arbiter of European affairs Russia had to keep a strong army. Thus the demonstration of military might became the chief expression of the political and social life of the Russian ruling class. This in turn required the architectural and spatial reorganization of the center to accommodate these military spectacles. The Marsovo Pole drill and parade grounds were located too far from the palace and furthermore proved inadequate because of their lack of proper approaches. It was therefore necessary to create a direct spatial relationship between the Winter Palace—at that time the official seat of the government—and the surrounding areas to provide an adequate physical setting for the grandiose military parades in which the most active unit was the "body

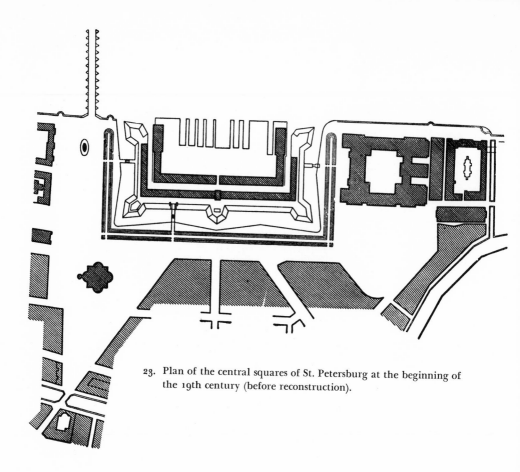

23. Plan of the central squares of St. Petersburg at the beginning of
the 19th century (before reconstruction).

guard of His Majesty," called "the pride and glory of Russia."

The construction of the new ministries and the need for large open spaces around the Winter Palace for military parades was, in the final analysis, the real reason for the creation of the ensemble of the central squares of St. Petersburg (see illustrations 23 and 24). The construction of Nevski Prospect proceeded concurrently with the replanning of the central area which was gradually transformed into a fully developed spatial composition by the introduction of a number of carefully placed link elements. As a result Nevski Prospect and its immediate vicinity were spatially (and archi-

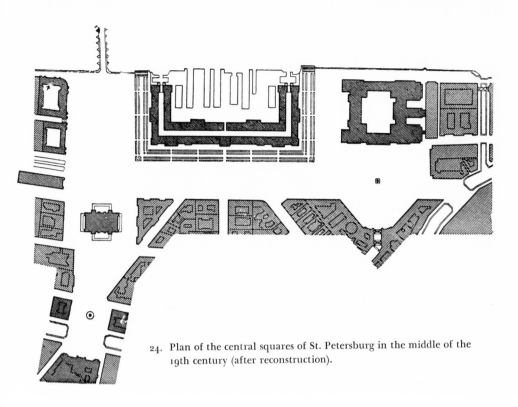

24. Plan of the central squares of St. Petersburg in the middle of the 19th century (after reconstruction).

tecturally) subordinated to the system of the central squares.

The organization of such a vast undertaking obviously called for a special coordinating agency, and in 1816 a building committee, the Committee of Construction and Hydraulic Works, was formed under the chairmanship of Lieutenant-General Betancourt. The decree ordering its establishment is interesting because, in addition to spelling out its administrative purpose, it goes on to enumerate the various problems which were to be solved by the architects and engineers engaged for the work of improving anything related to the further development of St. Petersburg.[6] This outline of the problems to be solved represented a comprehensive program for the future development of the central area in all its technical and civic aspects. The ukase specified that ". . . government buildings, private houses, and all other structures within the capital should be of good design. Furthermore, they should receive constant additional care for their good maintenance and possible improvement." The same document went on to point out the necessity for "taking into consideration the function, beauty, and the propriety of each building with respect to the whole city" and the "advantageous siting, the structural stability, and the functional integrity of each individual building in harmony with both its neighbors and the whole environment." The ukase further clarified the reasons for the appointment of the committee:

> . . . in order that all the above shall be properly taken into consideration according to the accepted rules of best architectural practice, and in order that the appearance of the buildings in the capital be raised to such beauty and perfection as to reflect in all their aspects its dignity and importance as the capital of a great empire, thus enhancing the general as well as the individual welfare of its citizens.

The members of the committee were the architects Rossi, Modiui, Stasov, and Mikhailov. Their duties as outlined by the ukase were as follows:

1. New building regulations for the proper control of all construction within the city limits were to be gradually introduced and all existing laws concerning building and construction to be reviewed.
2. In the future all plans for proposed new buildings erected within the city limits were to be submitted to the planning authority. This affected public as well as private structures.
3. A comprehensive study of the existing sewer system and all other hydraulic works was to be made. This was to in-

clude a description of their present condition as well as proposals describing in detail the methods to be employed for the cleaning of all sewers, and their future protection from obstruction. Other proposals were to be made describing alternative methods for the construction of overpasses, bridges, etc.

The decree also ordered "a complete review of all existing planning proposals and any other material pertaining to the existing state of the city." Any of these which appeared to be of use were to be explored and noted. The following guidelines were to be followed:

1. The termination of all proposed streets in the most attractive manner, and according to current best practices.
2. The planning of new streets, where necessary, for convenient circulation, according to the best fire-prevention practices.
3. The gradual aligning of existing street fronts in the course of all future reconstruction works, since they do not at the present conform to any established setbacks or street line restrictions.
4. The reconstruction of old squares, and the creation of new ones, wherever these are deemed necessary and useful.
5. The establishment of public buildings as well as other structures around these squares, in harmony with the character of the locality, but also conforming to the needs of industry, and for the maximum benefit and pleasure of the public.
6. The opening of new passages near the river banks, where these are at the present inadequate for their purpose, taking into account the need for new bridges which would reduce the length of communication links.

The committee was further instructed to "prepare special rules and standard drawings and details for the design, structure, accommodations, layout, use, climatic orientation, and general function of all future new government buildings to be erected in the city of St. Petersburg."

It can be seen from the above that the committee was invested with great responsibility and almost unlimited powers of control over all the construction in the city. Fortunately, it was composed of very highly qualified professionals with Betancourt as its head and some of the best architects of the period on its staff. The supervision of the reconstruction works was thus in good hands. Unfortunately, the Committee of Construction and Hydraulic Works was unable to make full use of its extensive powers. For example, it very often happened that drawings of important projects which had been approved and checked by the imperial court and which had great significance for the proper development of the ensemble of the central squares and Nevski Prospect were routed so as to bypass the committee. This happened, for instance, during the reconstruction of Dvortsovaia Square and also during the construction of the Mikhailovski Palace and the Alexander Theater, i.e., those projects which were executed by the building commissions attached directly to the Tsar's Cabinet.

All the projects passing through the hands of these building commissions—beginning with the planning of the separate ensembles and ending with the interior layout of the individual buildings—had to be approved by Alexander I personally and, after his death, by Nikolai I. After a project had been approved or rejected by the Tsar no committee could alter anything in opposition to His Majesty's "highest will." Very often the Committee of Construction and Hydraulic Works did not even receive a copy of the approved plan. The archives are full of requests by the committee for copies of the drawings of buildings already under construction so that they could be plotted on the general plan of St. Petersburg.

In this connection a letter by the military governor-general of St. Petersburg, M. Milopadovin, to one of the ministers of H. M. Cabinet is characteristic:

> . . . certain projects under the jurisdiction of the commission could not be inspected by the "committee," for the simple reason that in recent times certain authorities have presented them directly to His Majesty for highest approval. The "committee" has therefore not even a copy of these projects and is unable to transfer the information gained from these drawings to the general plan of St. Petersburg. In order to prevent the recurrence of such difficulties in the future I humbly beg Your Eminence to issue instructions to have sent to my office a copy of all the plans and projects which have been approved by His Highness, and which have not been previously inspected, in order that these may be conveyed to the committee for study.[7]

The fact that the Committee of Construction and Hydraulic Works was bypassed in the approval of large scale projects that were important to the overall development of the central ensemble limited its full effectiveness as a planning body. But there is no doubt that it did a great deal in connection with the remaining volume of construction, namely, the "fillers" between the main complexes of the city. Here the committee regulated and controlled the siting, the character of the façades, and the general height of the buildings, as well as their street alignment.

There was no general plan for the reconstruction of the area of the central squares. Their development was carried out piecemeal, and many eminent designers participated in this task. It is generally believed that Rossi did all the planning for the central area, but careful studies by P. Stolpianski refute this assumption,[8] as the following indicates:

> On July 4, 1824, the Secretary of State, and confidential advisor, Senator Kikin informed the minister of the interior that his Imperial Highness, Tsar Alexander I, had

given his royal consent to the request of the Venetian noblemen Antoine de Rossi, who proposed to build a scale model of the royal city of St. Petersburg, and, in order to be able to proceed with its construction, he applied for a ten year "privilege" and exemption from all taxes.

The model was built in the following manner: the general staff supplied A. de Rossi with an accurate map of St. Petersburg which he redrew on a considerably larger scale (1 arshin on the plan represented 240 arshins of actual measurement). This plan was then transferred to a number of boards which made up the base of the model. Each board measured 2 square arshins, for easy handling. All buildings of the city were reproduced from nature, showing not only their front façades facing the street, but also their rear, together with all their colonnades and other architectural adornments. The scale models of the buildings were made of cardboard; the roofs were made of lead; and the bridges and colonnades were made of wood. The Neva and the canals were represented by white tin and all statues were reproduced in alabaster.

The St. Petersburg architect, K. I. Rossi, helped Antoine Rossi with the organization of the work for the model. The architects Kavos and Buia worked on the composition of the model.[9]

The press of the day noted the high quality of the model:

It is impossible to describe the faithfulness of the architectural details; everything is made with utmost precision: The columns, the capitals, the façades, the balconies, the iron railings and the fences, the statues and even the color of the houses are accurately copied; thus each citizen of St. Petersburg is able to recognize not only the exterior façade of his own house, but also the details of the outhouses and the courts which are faithfully copied and reproduced exactly to scale.[10]

It was therefore not a question of a planning project, but of a model, reproducing the existing conditions of St. Petersburg in the first quarter of the 19th century. The model was not made by the architect Karl Rossi but by his namesake Antoine de Rossi.[11]

This strongly supports the contention that the large reconstruction works in the center of St. Petersburg were being carried out without a general comprehensive plan or any definite architectural guidance in the formal sense. However, this does not mean that there was no general, overall concept for the development of the ensemble. The great skill of the masters who designed the various parts of the central ensemble was directed toward the integration of each separate project within the overall system of the whole central area of St. Petersburg.

In the year 1819, and concurrently with other major city building works, such as the redevelopment of the Strelka, the reconstruction of the Admiralty, and the erection of the Kazan Cathedral, documents, later found in the so-called *Archive Meier,* included a number of measures to be carried out in connection with the reconstruction of the ensemble of the five central squares.

The following were those concerning Dvortsovaia Square:

1. Tear down the corner of the existing building of the General Staff. [This concerns the demolition of the sharp angular corner projecting into Dvortsovaia Square near Lugovaia Street, where the arch was later built.]
2. Arrange opposite façades to be symmetrical. [Symmetrical to the building designed by I. M. Feldten.]
3. Purchase all the houses up to the Parade Grounds.
4. Build a bridge across the Moika [future Pevcheski Bridge near Dvortsovaia Square].
5. Define the space and function of the square behind St. Isaac Cathedral.

There were also some directives concerning Nevski Prospect:

6. Organize Nikolaevski Square. [The square in front of the Anichkov Palace which at that time belonged to the brother of the Emperor Nikolai and is now called Ostrovski Square.]
7. Construct a theater on the same square.
8. Construct a library on the same square.
9. Purchase all houses behind St. Kazan Cathedral.
10. Erect a matching colonnade on the other side of St. Kazan Cathedral.
11. Construct a central mall along Nevski Prospect.
12. Construct the Mikhailovski Palace.[12]

Thus almost all the large projects such as the Alexander Theater, the Mikhailovski Palace, Dvortsovaia Square, and St. Isaac Square, realized in the second quarter of the 19th century, were already planned by 1819.

The reconstruction works which were undertaken within the center of St. Petersburg in the first half of the 19th century reflect one of the most exceptional periods in the history of city building. Apart from some mistakes and minor deficiencies, the finished work is a brilliant example of the mastery and accomplishment of Russian urbanism in the 19th century. It is unsurpassed in scope, in the variety of the work accomplished, and in the clarity of its spatial concept.

6

The reconstruction of the Admiralty Building

The first major project within the area of the future ensemble of the five central squares was the reconstruction of the Admiralty carried out in the years 1806 to 1823. There were several reasons for starting the project at that particular time. The year 1805 was the centenary of the founding of the Admiralty by Peter I, and naturally the question of how to commemorate the occasion of this anniversary arose. The Admiralty Council established by Peter I was reorganized in 1802 in line with the formation of the other new ministries and was subsequently renamed the Ministry of Naval Forces. The new ministry expanded with the rest of the military establishment and needed more suitable accommodations. The appearance of the old building shocked everybody in St. Petersburg, indeed, with the exception of the entrance gate and the tower, the old Admiralty (see illustration 25) presented a rather dilapidated and drab sight: "The building consisted of many disparate sections of two and three stories respectively, with endless rows of windows, dull in appearance and bare in comparison with the other ornate buildings of Alexander I's capital." [1]

At the beginning of 1806, A. Zakharov was commissioned to design a new façade for the Admiralty. On May 16, the project was ready and was submitted to the Admiralty. On the same day Admiral F. Ushakov presented the drawings to the Tsar.[2] Alexander I approved the project on May 23, 1806, and actual work was started that year.

No official schedule guided the sequence of the reconstruction works in the central area of St. Petersburg—mainly because under the given conditions it was difficult to prepare one—the sequence being determined by rather accidental factors. The reconstruction of the old Admiralty was in this case a fortunate and apt beginning. Its central location within the territory of the Admiralty District, its architectural and visual links with the major circulation elements of the city, and its significance in the formal definition of the three central squares and the waterfront of the Neva made it imperative that reconstruction be started here.

Any objective evaluation of Zakharov's design must begin with the understanding that he did not design a new building. The building department attached to the Admiralty Council was in fact called the Office for the Reconstruction of the Admiralty Façades. Zakharov wrote the following explanatory note about the project:

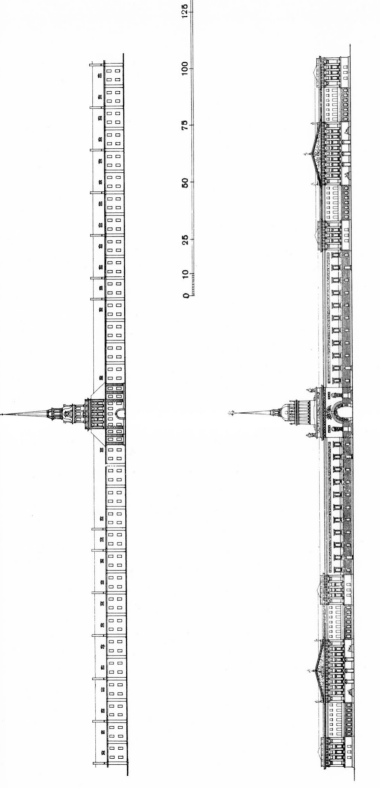

25. Top: Admiralty designed by I. K. Korobov (built 1732–1738).
Bottom: Admiralty reconstruction by A. D. Zakharov (built 1806–1820).

During the design of the project I made it a rule to retain as many of the good features of the old building as possible. This in turn impelled me to prevent the tearing down of existing walls which could be used, and to utilize the existing foundations wherever it was feasible and safe. As a result, only a few new walls had to be added.[3]

In the process of its design and construction it became inevitable that a number of urban design problems had to be considered as well. The first one concerned the location of the Admiralty within the spatial structure of the central area of the city. The singularity of its location was the result of the convergence of five major boulevards upon the central complex of the Admiralty, namely the two quays—Dvortsovaia and Angliiskaia quays—and the three radial boulevards—Nevski Prospect, Voznesenski Prospect and Gorokhovaia Street. All of these emanated from different parts of the city, and all of them ultimately found their termination at the Admiralty. In terms of their spatial and visual aspects these five boulevards pointed toward the main focal element of the city center. This called for a strong architectural articulation at their point of convergence. Due to the different spatial dispositions of these five arteries, two separate design problems had to be solved since the termination of the radials called for a different architectural solution than the termination of the quays.

The system of the "three prongs" converged upon the Admiralty by means of its three radials and their common point of termination was defined by the tower. The termination of the two quays represented a different design problem and will be discussed later. The architectural articulation at the point of convergence of the three radials had already been solved successfully in Peter I's time, and it was later reinforced even more by Ivan Korobov during the first reconstruction of the Admiralty in the years 1734–1735 (see illustration 26). The old Admiralty Tower was indisputably the most successful feature of the whole composition. Adrian Zakharov was thus faced with the problem of incorporating the old tower into the design of his new façade. The solution to this problem was the most complex and difficult aspect of the whole design. The tower was not only part of the general façade of the Admiralty complex, but due to its singular spatial position it also became an element of enormous spatial and architectural importance within the system of the three radials and, by extension, the whole area of the central ensemble.

Let us first examine the tower as conceived by I. Korobov and then make a comparison with the new design of A. Zakharov. The old tower design consisted of two distinct architectural elements. The horizontal masses of the main wings and their transition to the tower represented the first element and the tower itself the second. The cube formed by the transition elements and the base of the tower rose above the squat masses of the substructure. The tower itself, almost square at its base, became gradually smaller toward the top and terminated in the spire, which in its elegance and simplicity of outline became the most successful feature of the old building. Zakharov had this to say concerning the tower:

> The gate below the spire should be increased in height; the foundation below the gate should be strengthened to support the additional walls; similarly the foundation of the tower itself should be reinforced. The spire should not be changed at all, except for the lantern and the details below the spire, all of which should receive an altogether new appearance.[4]

In retaining the graceful spire with the golden ship at the top and changing the design of the lower part, Zakharov obvi-

27. The Admiralty Tower after reconstruction, after a drawing by Zakharov.

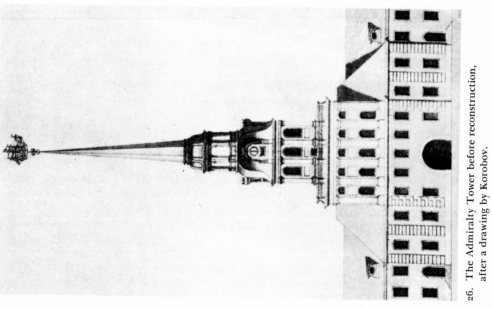

26. The Admiralty Tower before reconstruction, after a drawing by Korobov.

ously did the right thing. Such a modification of Korobov's original composition was certainly well justified.

One of the deficiencies of the old tower was its weak articulation in regard to the general mass of the building. The need to remedy this became an absolute necessity, since, apart from its aspect as part of the Admiralty façade, the tower also had to be considered as an integral part of the central ensemble and furthermore as the focal point of the "three prongs." The only way to accomplish this was to make the tower an independent architectural element within the overall composition of the Admiralty façade. The tower is visible through the gap at the end of each of the three long perspectives of the radial avenues. It was therefore of great importance that this gap be filled by a clearly defined architectural terminal element. Korobov's tower was not overly successful in this respect: it did not project forward far enough to be visually separate from the rest of the façade. Its slight projection forward was scarcely noticeable from a distance, and the continuous cornice line—which was the same for all parts of the building— made a visual separation of the tower mass from the rest of the building even more difficult. In the long perspectives of the boulevards it was difficult to perceive the old tower as a clearly defined focal element. Instead, it appeared as a fragment of a larger whole cut off from the rest by the edges of the buildings at the end of the perspectives.

In contrast to Korobov's design, Zakharov increased the base of the tower, at the same time making the best use of the existing foundation walls of the old central part of the building (see illustration 27). As a result, the lower part of the new tower almost entirely fills the gap at the end of the perspective view from the Moika along any of the three radial boulevards. In order to achieve a clear articulation of the central part even at close range—where the tower could be seen together with the sidewings—and in order to avoid the mistakes made by Korobov, whose tower merged visually with the rest of the building, Zakharov interrupted the main cornice line. He lifted the central part above the height of the sidewings, and differentiated it even more by changing its architectural detail. This added enormously to the articulation of the tower as an independent architectural element.

The process of Zakharov's thinking is made apparent by his preliminary sketches. In the early sketches the projection of the tower beyond the main façade of the sidewings is almost imperceptible. The original scheme still maintains a continuous cornice line for both the tower and the two sidewings. In the final version, however, he changed all this and there are no more transitional elements between the main body of the building and the tower except the lower part, which helps to relate the vertical central element to the horizontals of the sidewings (see illustration 27). The critic V. I. Kurbatov commented on all this as follows:

> With the exception of the base, the whole central part was left smooth, thus giving the tower an independent architectural character. The designer may have avoided monotony by these devices, but he committed a worse blunder by disrupting the organic continuity of the overall design.[5]

However, it was by no means exclusively a question of breaking the monotony of the façade. Not only did Zakharov succeed in relieving the overall monotony of the long frontal elevation but he also provided a strong visual termination for the "three prongs" in the central area of St. Petersburg. This was achieved by making the tower an architecturally independent element of the overall architectural composition. Zakharov's great architectural skill is demonstrated by the fact that he fully comprehended the visual relationship between the Admiralty Tower and the system of the radials. He recognized the proper design priorities, thus solving the problem boldly and with great conceptual clarity.

As one looked toward the center along any one of the three radials the general outline of the Admiralty Tower against the sky was of great visual importance. Seen from a distance details get lost, nuances disappear, the intensity of light decreases, and the general outline usually becomes more important. In terms of these considerations, the silhouette of the old tower was quite successful. Its main drawback was its baroque complexity, which expressed itself in a picturesque manner whereby one flowing line joined with another without clear or definite articulation. In defense of Korobov it may be said that he did not expect the tower to be viewed from a great distance since in his time St. Petersburg extended only as far as the Fontanka. However, by 1806 the city had grown considerably, and the silhouette of the tower had to be expressed in a much more powerful way to be effective. Its outlines had to be made simple, clear, and strong.

Looking along Nevski Prospect from its farthest point on a clear day, one can clearly perceive below the entrance arches the two sculptural groups, the bas-relief details along the frieze, the columns set off by deep shadows, and, above all, the gilded needle of the elegant spire rising above the rest. Each part is related formally to the next in such a way as to achieve maximum spatial contrast. Everything is based on clear contrast such as solid against hollow and straightline against curvilinear. Everything is calculated to read clearly from a great distance. At this point a few words about the details may be in order. As one looked toward Korobov's old Admiralty along Nevski Prospect, no single detail of the building was dramatic enough to arouse the spectator's interest and to entice him to seek out the tower. It was possible to guess all of its main features from a moderate distance. In contrast to this, Zakharov's tower attracts the spectator from any distance—near or far. Stepping closer, one's curiosity is amply rewarded. The details reveal the function of the building. Bas-reliefs depict the founding of the Russian fleet and the heroic deeds of Russian sailors. In contrast, the details of Korobov's old tower were of a strictly tectonic nature and devoid of any descriptive themes.

The question of scale and scale relationships also warrants discussion. In the usual sense of the word architectural scale is defined as the relationship between the building and the human figure. If one were asked to draw a human figure on the elevational drawings made by Korobov and Zakharov respectively, one would find that the figure would be of a different size in each case, larger on the elevation designed by Zakharov, smaller on the one designed by Korobov. In the drawing of the old Admiralty Tower the size of the human figure may be easily related to the size of the windows and the balustrades, and any error made on the basis of such a comparison would be relatively small. The task is much more difficult in the case of Zakharov's drawing. It seems that he intentionally distorted the scale by eliminating all those detail elements which relate to human size. Anyone attempting to judge the size of the human figure by relating it to the size of the entrance arch or the scale of the sculptural groups would end up by making a considerable mistake. Thus Adrian Zakharov's design is purposely not related to the scale of the human figure, as was Korobov's old tower, but to the large spaces of the surrounding ensemble of the central area of St. Petersburg.

The scale of the central ensemble was indeed closely related to the features of the site, to the size of the islands, and to the large water surfaces of the Neva. The first designer who understood this monumental scale relationship was

Domenico Trezzini. From the interior of the fortress, the spire of the Peter and Paul Cathedral seems to be out of scale with respect to the rest of the cathedral, but looking across the river from Dvortsovaia Quay one begins to understand the reason for this apparent scale discrepancy. Such great masters as P. Eropkin, who completed the planning of the "three prongs," and Rastrelli, who designed the Smolny Monastery and the Winter Palace, understood this larger scale relationship which was dictated by the features of the landscape and the overall structural and spatial system of the city. They used this monumental scale to best advantage both in the planning of the various parts of the city and in the design of its individual buildings.

The following is a description of the structural devices used by Zakharov to achieve his design while at the same time saving as much of the existing structure as possible. Illustration 28 shows that the master proceeded with great technical skill, adding new walls only where it was absolutely necessary while at the same time skillfully incorporating the structural frame of the old building into the new design. In spite of the great care taken by the architect, actual construction did not proceed without difficulties.

The integration of the old walls with the new ones and the construction of the new arch above the gate—placed on the existing foundations—required professional daring and great technical skill. Nevertheless, certain factors could not be anticipated. In 1814, soon after the death of Zakharov, a number of cracks appeared in the tower walls. These cracks were caused by differential settlement of the combined foundation walls. In reply to anxious inquiries by the ministry, the superintendent of building, R. Diergard, a professional engineer, had this to say:

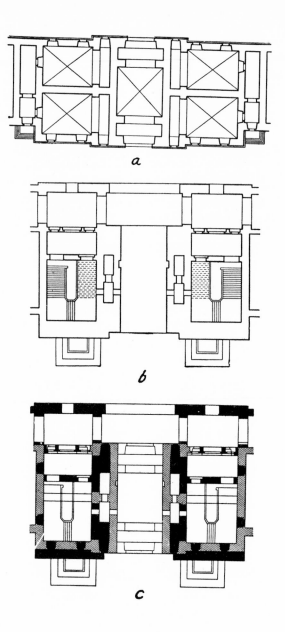

28. Plans of the Admiralty Tower; a. before reconstruction; b. after
reconstruction; c. old and new walls (old hatched, new black).

The newly formed cracks in the walls should not be considered dangerous to the structural integrity of the building as indeed this is unavoidable in a building where new walls have been added to old ones. . . . I can assure Your Excellency of my personal confidence in this matter, particularly in view of the fact that from the very beginning . . . the new façade of the building was erected under the personal supervision of the great master Zakharov. By skillfully joining the spandrel of the new arch above the main gate to the old walls of the former building Zakharov accomplished a remarkable structural feat. By means of the new arch the heavy loads of the new superstructure were more equally distributed and even now one cannot help but admire the skill with which this difficult structural problem was solved . . . without disturbing the rest of the structure.[6]

The first architectural task, namely the visual termination of the radials and the creation of a focal element at their point of convergence, was solved by Zakharov with great success.

The sidewings of the Admiralty provided the visual termination of Dvortsovaia Quay from one side and of Angliiskaia Quay from the other. Dvortsovaia Quay entered Razvodnaia Square on the eastern side while Angliiskaia Quay joined up with Senate Square in the west. In the first half of the 19th century these two quays were not yet connected with one another. In order to reach Dvortsovaia Quay from Angliiskaia Quay, it was necessary to walk all the way around the Admiralty. Thus, the sidewings of the Admiralty provided not only the first glimpse of the large complex from either side of the quays, but at the same time provided for their respective architectural and visual termination. The design of the sidewings was not completed without obstacles, and for a full understanding of this aspect of Zakharov's design it is necessary to relate an incident which occurred during their construction and which resulted in a change of the architect's original plans.

According to the original scheme, the sidewings were supposed to be built much closer to the Neva in line with the other buildings along the quays. The wing of the Admiralty on the side of the Winter Palace had almost been completed when Zakharov was suddenly ordered to appear at the court of Alexander I. The audience took place on June 2, 1808. In a report sent to Minister Yagarov on the following day, Zakharov wrote:

> It appears that the corners of the Admiralty wings are projecting out too far toward the river thus obstructing the view from the royal chambers of the Winter Palace toward Galernaia Quay and the estuary of the Neva. His Royal Highness has therefore issued an order to remove that part of the building which is obstructing the view . . . it will be necessary to pull the building back 9 sazhen [21 feet] from its original position, for which purpose markers have been placed showing the old position of the building as originally called for in the plans and also its new limits, taking into account the view. These markers can be perceived from the windows of His Royal Highness' chambers.[7]

On June 17 Zakharov submitted a revised plan for royal approval, which was promptly given. He did not change the general design of the elevation but merely pulled the building back 18 meters [37 feet] from the edge of the Neva.

Had the original design been carried out, the sidewings of the Admiralty would have lined up with the rear edge of the Winter Palace facing the Neva. Their short ends would have been in line with the palace façade and would thus not have been visible from the two quays. Actually, such a position directly at the edge of the river would neither have accomplished a direct closure of the perspective views from the two quays (which in the final analysis could not be considered an absolute necessity) nor would it have provided the proper architectural closure for the quays. To accomplish this, it would have been necessary either to project the wings beyond the general line of the buildings along the waterfront or to recess them, using the side elevations of the Winter Palace and the Senate Building beyond as the terminating elements of the two quays. The latter alternative was eventually realized. Thus Alexander I's whim ended up having positive consequences for the architectural improvement of the central ensemble.

In order to go from Dvortsovaia Quay to Angliiskaia Quay one had to pass around the front of the Admiralty Building, which represented a distance of over 800 feet. This was naturally considered highly inconvenient. At the beginning of the 19th century proposals were made to connect the two quays by means of a passage behind the Admiralty. Inasmuch as it was possible to predict that this would eventually be done—in which case the Neva waterfront would be converted into a continuous thoroughfare from Liteiny Dvor to Galerni Harbor—the special significance of the Admiralty sidewings as architectural terminating elements of the two quays became redundant. In the light of this new situation, the fact that they were recessed into the depth of the shore actually turned out to be an advantage, since it was now possible to catch an oblique glimpse of their short elevations facing the Neva from each of the two quays.

As far as the architectural expression of the sidewings is concerned they were—like the tower—independent and complete architectural compositions, well related to the general architectural organization of the total ensemble.

The tower and the sidewings unquestionably belonged to the system of squares around the Admiralty and were thus an integral part of the spatial structure of the central ensemble of St. Petersburg. However, apart from the above, Zakharov also had to deal with other design problems. One of these was the formal treatment of the new Admiralty façades which faced the three surrounding large squares.

It must not be forgotten that the old Admiralty was originally a fortress, surrounded by fairly high earth moats, and that the surrounding area was part of the so-called Admiralty Green which was at that time still very poorly developed. While in Zakharov's time the outlines of Admiralty Square itself were already quite well defined, both Dvortsovaia and Senate squares were then without any definite architectural organization. During the reconstruction of the Admiralty, the surrounding buildings and squares (with the exception of the Winter Palace) were still incomplete in the architectural sense. In this respect, then, the new Admiralty "set the stage" for the newly emerging central ensemble of the city.

In the articulation of the architectural masses of the main façade Zakharov anticipated the spatial significance of the future squares surrounding the complex. Disregarding the tower, which properly belongs to the system of the radials, Zakharov placed all the other main architectural accents near the ends of the principal elevation. In this way he predetermined the significance of the future Admiralty Square as an intermediate circulation link between Dvortsovaia Square and Senate Square.

However, it is equally possible that Zakharov did not anticipate all this at the time of the reconstruction of the Admiralty, and that the design of the porticoes as separately articulated elements of the façade may merely have reflected the desire to create a contrast between the long horizontal main body of the building and the verticality of the richly decorated tower. Whichever the case, the breaking up of the main façade and the architectural articulation of the separate axial elements of the composition related very well to the spatial significance of the individual squares within the general context of the fully developed future central ensemble.

From one of Zakharov's early sketches it can be inferred that the idea of a single space containing five mutually connected squares was conceived only later (see illustration 29). This sketch is highly important for a proper understanding of the future architectural development of the ensemble. It shows that at this point the old defense system around the Admiralty was still an integral part of the overall design. In his successive schemes he made other similar proposals, which showed the Admiralty surrounded by bastions and a canal, with a boulevard passing in front and parallel to the main façade of the building. If these schemes had been realized the whole Admiralty complex would have taken up a considerable part of the future central squares and would have dominated the adjacent spaces to a much larger degree. Obviously, this would have precluded the formation of Razvodnaia Square as well as Admiralty Square, and Senate Square would have been reduced to a mere passage. Thus the implementation of Zakharov's original scheme would have seriously disrupted the spatial continuity of the open squares around the Admiralty (see illustration 29).

Insofar as the Admiralty was conceived as an island complex, surrounded by a canal and fronted by a boulevard, Zakharov had some reason to treat the architectural integration of the Admiralty with the surrounding buildings as of secondary importance. However, the plan of 1806 was not realized. Later, when the parades in honor of Russian victories became a weekly affair in St. Petersburg, it was decided to reorganize the center of the city to accommodate them.

During the period of the European Congress, parades and reviews in Russia as well as abroad singularly occupied the

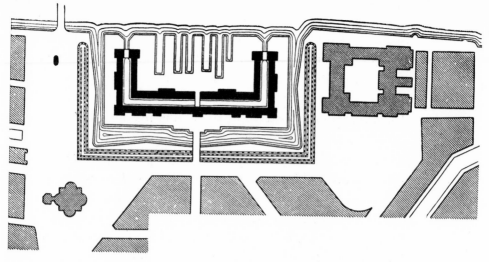

29. The Admiralty and its immediate vicinity according to Zakharov's original scheme.

mind of Tsar Alexander I. . . . In St. Petersburg parades were held on the following days: on the day of Bogoiavlenia-Kreshchenski; on March 13 in memory of the battle of Fer-Champ; on March 19, the day of the conquest of Paris; on May Day; the summer parade on August 17 in memory of the battle of Kulm, and the autumn and winter parades. Apart from the preceding ones, further parades were held for special occasions, such as the parade in honor of the arrival of Prussian potentates in St. Petersburg. Finally many parades were held in honor of each return of Alexander I to the capital from his many tours of Russia and abroad after the end of the congress as well as before each departure of the Tsar for any one of his numerous tours.[8]

These spectacles required the widening of the passage in front of the Admiralty and the demolition of the old fortification works around the Admiralty, thus preventing the implementation of Zakharov's original scheme. Some demolition of the old fortification works had already been started during the first years of the reconstruction. Reports found in old Admiralty files reveal that:

. . . following a suggestion made by the chief architect Zakharov . . . part of the wall around the Admiralty, which was situated at an angle to the Winter Palace and opposite Nevski Prospect, obstructed the free movement of building materials . . . whereupon he entered a request for the removal of this portion of the wall.[9]

Soon after, the decision was made to cancel the construction of the new fortifications as well as of the canal and the bridges, all of which had been included in Zakharov's original scheme. Zakharov has this to say about the abandonment of the fortification works:

I was very fortunate . . . to receive His Majesty's command . . . concerning the draining and filling of the Admiralty canal . . . and after the completion of these works . . . to proceed with the reconstruction of the leveled area in an appropriate and tasteful manner.[10]

The demolition of the old fortifications was instrumental in the formation of Admiralty Square and Razvodnaia Square and effectively changed the spatial disposition of the various elements in the future system of the five central squares. Their removal created a new architectural relationship between the newly opened space and the Admiralty complex. In Zakharov's original scheme the Admiralty Building represented the main architectural and spatial element within the central complex. Now in addition to its new functional purpose, the spatial significance of the large square in front of the Admiralty increased and the huge central mass of the Admiralty took on the role of its peripheral architectural boundary (see illustration 30). With the opening of the square the architectural and spatial importance of all the surrounding buildings took on an entirely new aspect. This, in turn, raised the question of the architectural treatment of the opposite sides of the square and the spatial relationships between the Ad-

The reconstruction of the Admiralty Building

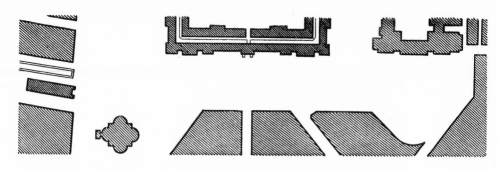

30. Top: The Admiralty and its immediate vicinity after the removal of the moat and the earth walls. Bottom: The method used for the determination of the width of Admiralty Boulevard, thus "adjusting" the position of the front elevation of the Riding Academy with respect to the long axis of the boulevard.

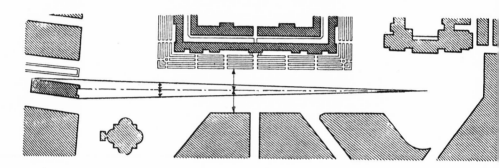

miralty and the buildings on the opposite side of Admiralty Square.

Razvodnaia Square is of some interest in this connection. It is faced by the Winter Palace on one side and the Admiralty on the other. The east wing of the Admiralty facing the Winter Palace anchors the square within the larger system of the other squares around it. Originally it was planned to bring the Admiralty wing into a simple architectural relationship with the palace elevation, maintaining the same length and the same central axis as the Winter Palace. However, a mere duplication of length and a common central axis would

not have been sufficient to bring about the architectural unification of the space. In a comparison of the two opposite
façades it becomes obvious that unfortunately Zakharov did
not give the problem as much thought as Feldten and, after
him, Rossi. Both were involved, at different periods of time,
with designing and redesigning the General Staff Building,
and they were certainly much more careful to relate it architecturally to the Winter Palace. The violation of the formal
architectural relationship between the palace and the sidewings of the Admiralty resulted from the Tsar's order to pull
them back from the Neva, and also from Zakharov's failure
to redesign the thus shortened façades. Instead, he decided
merely to decrease the intermediate portion between the end
porticoes. As a result, Razvodnaia Square was faced by two
important monumental buildings which did not possess the
same high architectural qualities as Dvortsovaia Square, designed by Rossi.

The large Admiralty Square was thus formed as a result of
the removal of the old earth fortifications in front of the
Admiralty. The creation of this new square opened up the
continuous space stretching from the Riding Academy of the
Konogvardeiski Regiment in the west to the end of Dvortsovaia Square in the east. This represented a distance of almost
1,000 meters [approx. 3,400 feet]. Thus, the central squares
were now all united into a single continuous large space.
Within this newly unified space the architectural relationships among the various individual buildings—including the
many aspects of their spatial juxtaposition—were obviously
subject to considerable change.

Before the reconstruction of the Admiralty Building, the
Riding Academy (designed by G. Quarenghi) provided the
visual termination of the view from the narrow passage south
of the old earth fortifications in front of the Admiralty. The

gate of the Riding Academy coincided with the central axis of the passage defining it architecturally. In Zakharov's original scheme the existence of this building posed no additional problems to the designer and had no new significance within the spatial structure of the overall plan.

After the formation of the new Admiralty Square, however, Quarenghi's Riding Academy attained a new and important spatial significance. Seen from the far end of Dvortsovaia Square the Riding Academy had now become the visual and architectural terminus of the whole vast space of the central squares. Within the context of strict geometrical regularity, which was the main characteristic of the central squares, the slight axial deviation of the Riding Academy from the main axis suddenly became very much apparent. Prior to the widening of the passage in front of the Admiralty this axial inclination was hardly noticeable. The high moats of the fortification works screened off most of the view and from the narrow passage only the front elevation of the building could be seen.

However, from the newly widened Admiralty Square the Riding Academy displayed not only its front but also a foreshortened view of its side. Thus, from the distance of Dvortsovaia Square, the outline of the whole bulk of the Riding Academy was visible, notwithstanding the fact that the deviation of its main axis from the long axis of the Admiralty Square was not very large. The Riding Academy was therefore the only element which did not fit into the rectilinear grid of the ensemble. To correct this condition, it was decided to do some "adjusting."

After the old Admiralty moat was filled in, in 1816, it was replaced by a wide boulevard which transformed the northern part of Admiralty Square into a two-way circulation link (see top of illustration 30). As a result the long axis of the remaining square was displaced further south, away from the Admiralty and closer to the central axis of the front façade of the Riding Academy. The apparent location of the longitudinal axis of the square was therefore determined by the geometric bisection of the width of the boulevard which, in turn, could be easily manipulated by the displacement of its northern edge. The exterior limit of the boulevard was therefore chosen in such a way as to make the axis of the square coincide with the bisection of a visual cone subtending the outlines of the front elevation of the Riding Academy (see bottom of illustration 30). This was the method used for "adjusting" the Riding Academy to the rectilinear grid of the new ensemble.

The creation of the new boulevard in front of the Admiralty served a number of additional functions. It helped to separate the large bulk of the Admiralty visually from the diverse masses of surrounding buildings. To some degree this represented an implementation of Zakharov's original scheme, even though the means were different. The moat and the earth walls were now replaced by the boulevard. In both cases the interjection of an intermediate spatial element made the architectural incoherence between the Admiralty and the surrounding buildings less noticeable. In order to connect the two quays on each side of the Admiralty, the boulevard turned toward the Neva along both of its sidewings, joining the quays at their termination. After the introduction of the boulevard the axis of the remaining clear space of Senate Square coincided with the main axis of symmetry of St. Isaac Cathedral. Owing to the creation of the new boulevard Admiralty Square had become both a spatial and a functional link between Senate Square and Dvortsovaia Square. It thereby enhanced their architectural and spatial significance within the overall system of the five large central squares. The designer of Admiralty Boulevard is unknown. It is remarkable, however, how much was achieved by this relatively inexpensive and simple change.

The Admiralty of Zakharov, the Exchange of Thomas de Thomon, and the Gornyi Institute of Voronikhin illustrate best the new principles applied to the architectural organization of the huge spaces in the central area of the capital. They filled the need for a limited number of monumental buildings dominating the surrounding building masses. In accordance with these new principles, described at the beginning of this chapter, these key projects were free-standing architectural entities, complete in themselves and clearly dominating the large spaces of the central ensemble. The front elevation of Zakharov's design was oriented toward the central area of the city and the radials, whereas the rear and side elevations were related to the quays and the Neva. The tower defined the true architectural center of gravity of the whole complex.

Returning to a previously mentioned assumption that Zakharov may not have been primarily concerned with the architectural relationship between the Admiralty and the surrounding buildings, the fact remains that—very much like Thomas de Thomon and A. Voronikhin—he did everything possible to differentiate the building from its immediate surroundings by using a variety of architectural devices such as novelty, monumentality, and contrasting architectural forms. All this would have been impossible during the preceding period and represented a completely new point of departure from the classicism of the 18th century. Comparing the Gornyi Institute and the old Exchange on the Strelka—which can be regarded as pure examples of 18th-century design—Zakharov's scheme for the reconstruction of the Admiralty reveals an infinitely more complex conceptual fabric.

The demolition of the old fortification walls around the Admiralty and the opening up of the space in front for "a new use" marked the beginning of a new phase in the architectural development of the center of St. Petersburg in the 19th century that was probably equal in importance to the replacement of Quarenghi's old Exchange by the new complex designed by Thomas de Thomon. Such modest and apparently insignificant changes eventually transformed the concepts which were applied to the development of the central ensemble of St. Petersburg if for no other reason than that they were the concrete expression of the changes that were transforming the social and political life of the capital. The large squares around the Winter Palace were unified as a result of the modification of Zakharov's original scheme for the siting of the Admiralty fortifications. Their unification was functionally justified in providing an appropriate stage for the frequent and large military parades held in St. Petersburg at that time.

As a result of all these factors, the squares became the most important spatial element of the whole central ensemble. The opening up of the space around the Admiralty, furthermore, revealed the lack of architectural coherence between it and the surrounding buildings. In the early years of the 19th century, until about 1812, the prevailing canons of classicism called for the creation of an ensemble with a "drawn-out center" together with a number of monumental complexes in important spatial locations, dominating their surroundings. Response to the need for a large architectural setting for the massive military parades within the central area of the city invalidated these principles, and the subsequent opening up

of the central spaces exposed their inherent architectural deficiencies.

The principal aim of all the future work within the area
of the five central squares was to relate the various projects
to each other and ultimately to the monumental façade of
Zakharov's Admiralty. This could no longer be achieved by
creating additional "continuous façades." There was now a
need for an entirely new planning approach which would
synthesize the urban design ideas of the 18th and the early
19th centuries.

A. Peter and Paul Fortress on Petersburg Island.

B. Angliiskaia Quay. To the right, the Winter Palace; to the left, across
the Neva, the Peter and Paul Fortress.

C. The "united façade" along the left bank of the Neva. Winter Palace
in the foreground.

D. View along the central radial, Gorokhovaia Street (now Dzerzhinski Street)
toward Admiralty Tower.

E. Detail of Neva embankments. Peter and Paul Fortress in background.

F. Winter Palace (left) and east wing of Admiralty (right).

G. View along Admiralty Boulevard as it enters Dvortsovaia Square. Note Alexander Column in background.

H. Dvortsovaia Square with Alexander Column in center and the General Staff Building in background.

I. Detail of west facade of the Winter Palace.

J. View along Neva embankment toward the rounded corner of the Senate
Building. East wing of Admiralty in the foreground.

K. St. Isaac Cathedral dominating skyline. West wing of Admiralty on the right. Buildings to the left, occupying the site of the old Admiralty Courtyard, were added during the 19th century.

M. View along Nevski Prospect toward Admiralty Tower.

L. West portico of St. Isaac Cathedral. On the right one of Rauch's
    columns described in the text.

N. The Fontanka late on a July night.

O. The Moika.

7

The reconstruction of Dvortsovaia Square

The reconstruction of the Admiralty had not yet been fully completed when two other important projects were started at the two opposite ends of the city center: K. Rossi [1] was commissioned to direct the reconstruction of Dvortsovaia Square, while A. Montferrand began the reconstruction of St. Isaac Cathedral.

In 1819 a new Commission for the Development of the Square Opposite the Winter Palace was formed. It is characteristic of the planning approach of this period that the commission was not merely instructed to redesign the General

Staff Building but was charged with reorganizing the space of the square itself.

In making his decisions about the replanning of Dvortso-vaia Square the architect, K. Rossi, had to take into account a large number of factors: the existing spatial structure of the square and its general condition before reconstruction, as well as the history of its development within the changing context of the aesthetic and stylistic principles elaborated by his predecessors—which in itself constituted a rich architectural heritage. For a full understanding both of the complexity of the task that confronted Rossi and of the way in which he tackled the architectural problems posed, it is necessary to consider briefly the previous development of Dvortsovaia Square.

Organization of the space of Dvortsovaia Square had first fallen to Rastrelli [2] in the course of designing the Winter Palace. He had proposed enclosing part of the large space of Admiralty Field by a semicircular colonnade (see illustration 31) in front of the Winter Palace. Indeed, the effect of the white marble of the colonnade against the green of Admiralty Field would have been quite striking, and was inspired by the existing example of such an arrangement in the main court of Tsarskoe Selo. But although this purely decorative proposal was never realized, not all of Rastrelli's ideas passed into oblivion. Many of them were destined to exert a considerable influence on the subsequent architectural development of the square.

In the years from 1766 to 1769, the Commission for Masonry Construction focused its full attention on the planning of Dvortsovaia Square. While preparing the plan for the whole central area of the city and after having decided to build over most of the open space of the old Admiralty Field, A. Kvasov had to determine the general plan of Dvortsovaia

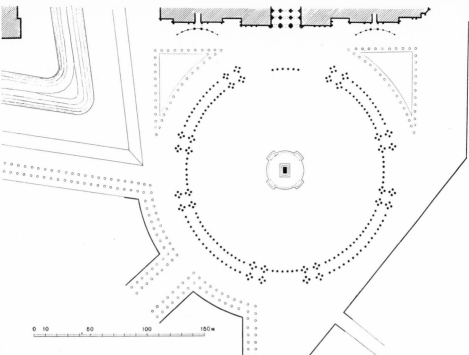

31. Proposed design for the square in front of the Winter Palace
(Dvortsovaia Square), with an equestrian statue of Peter I in the
center, by B. F. Rastrelli, 1753.

Square. The plan for this project—approved by Catherine II
in 1766 and again in 1769—shows the manner in which the
Commission for Masonry Construction intended to develop
the square.[3] It was conceived as an enclosed space architecturally separated from the rest of the ensemble. The plan reveals Rastrelli's influence both in the shape and the overall
spatial organization of the square.

After Nevski Prospect had been developed according to the
general plan, the urgent need to build up the sections facing
the square became apparent for the simple reason that most
of the back yards of the newly built residential buildings could
be seen from the windows of the Winter Palace. In 1779 the
Academy of Arts announced a competition for the design and
replanning of Dvortsovaia Square:

The reconstruction of Dvortsovaia Square

. . . the Academy of Arts invites all architects . . . to submit their ideas concerning the façades . . . which are to be
designed in harmony with this particular location, keeping
in mind that they will be erected directly opposite the palace
of Her Majesty.[4]

The Academy was aware of the many problems that had to
be solved, taking into account the general spatial structure of
the ensemble, and its members certainly realized the importance that Dvortsovaia Square took on due to its location opposite the royal palace. The competitors were urged ". . . to
secure plans of the existing buildings from the Academy of
Arts . . . for their further instruction and in order to arrive
at a better understanding of the problem." The competitors
were further limited by the conditions of the general plan
which had been previously prepared by the Commission for
Masonry Construction and which had won royal approval in
1769.

The actual plan for Dvortsovaia Square was conceived by
A. Kvasov who was a member of the commission. Strictly
speaking, the competition was intended merely to produce a
suitable design for the façades of the buildings facing the
square opposite the Winter Palace. Iu. M. Feldten received
the first prize and the curve originally proposed by Kvasov
was executed according to Feldten's design. However, this particular solution, conceived in plan by Kvasov and given architectural form by Feldten, was considered less than satisfactory
by their critics. The buildings along Lugovaia Street were
extremely diverse and unrelated to each other and their relationship to the new structures of Dvortsovaia Square was very
unsatisfactory. An undated plan for the improvement of
Dvortsovaia Square, found in the Hermitage, shows the buildings designed by Feldten superimposed on a plan which had
been drawn up by I. Starov.[5] The basic idea of Starov's pro-

posal was to hide the irregular outline of the buildings on the south side of the square by a free-standing, semicircular colonnade. Starov's proposal was not realized, and until the general reconstruction of all the five central squares, Dvortsovaia Square remained substantially unchanged.

At the beginning of the 19th century the plan and architectural organization of the square did not reflect the importance of its central location near the Winter Palace, nor did it express its spatial significance in the overall system of the central squares. The general plan reveals many of these deficiencies. After its final reconstruction the Winter Palace—apart from being the largest palace complex of the capital—had become one of the most beautiful buildings in the center of the city. The enormous size of the Admiralty, and the huge mass of the Peter and Paul Fortress, prompted Rastrelli to use a monumental scale which was in harmony with the large water surface of the river basin, and which seemed to anticipate the new spatial module of the future ensemble of the five central squares. The large open surfaces of the Neva, together with the wide sweep of the radials were spatial determinants well understood by Rastrelli. They were given architectural expression in his highly complex but nevertheless superbly balanced design of the elevations of the Winter Palace.

As mentioned before, the buildings along Lugovaia Street were out of scale with respect to the other buildings surrounding the square. These deficiencies were already quite evident in the early days of the 19th century. The existing buildings were not only of different height and size, but each of them represented a different architectural design. As a result of all this the whole block had the appearance of a confused and chaotic mass.

The second deficiency of the square was its lack of spatial

balance. Feldten's building, which had one main cornice, was four stories high, its overall height and massing corresponding to that of the Winter Palace. The buildings along Lugovaia Street had varying floor heights but were generally much lower. Although there was no clearly expressed axis of symmetry in the elevation of the Winter Palace, the violation of the spatial equilibrium by the disorganized architectural masses on the other side of the square was nevertheless clearly evident. Many drawings and etchings of that period confirm this.

The third architectural deficiency was the way in which Lugovaia Street entered the square. In his original project Rastrelli had made the entry of the street coincide with the central axis of the Winter Palace. In addition to this, it must be kept in mind that in Rastrelli's scheme the exit of Lugovaia Street was well within the general territory of the old Admiralty Field and thus did not enter into the spatial structure of the square itself, which was to be formed and defined by the proposed semicircular colonnades. In his planning proposal for Dvortsovaia Square, A. Kvasov obviously was unable to accept this layout, since this would have created an additional triangular space within the already fragmentary structure of the square.

In 1819 it was decided to correct the many architectural deficiencies of the square. It was also proposed that all the buildings on the south side of the square opposite the Winter Palace be reconstructed. In the early years of the 19th century Dvortsovaia Square became quite important in the life of the city. During the time of Catherine II it was used as a circulation link and a boulevard for coaches. Architecturally, it was fully subservient to the large mass of the Winter Palace. However, after its transformation into a parade ground it acquired an altogether new and independent spatial significance. As a result of this change, the juxtaposition of its constituent spatial elements also changed. The open space of the square became the dominant element while the surrounding buildings merely acted as its architectural frame.

The various architectural tasks connected with the reconstruction of Dvortsovaia Square can be formulated as follows. First, it was necessary to make the space of the square its dominant element, at the same time connecting it architecturally with the other large spaces of the central ensemble. Secondly, its function as a stage for huge military parades had to be given a proper architectural setting so that it would reflect the severe and grandiose character of the martial spectacles taking place within it. Architecturally this was achieved by monumentality and rigid control of detail. Finally, the new buildings around the square had to form a unified architectural whole with the large complex of the Winter Palace. The only limiting condition in the reconstruction of the square was the requirement that the buildings designed by Feldten—which gave the square its odd shape—be retained.

In 1819 the great architect, K. Rossi, started his work on the reconstruction of Dvortsovaia Square. The main features of his plan were determined by the existing curve of Feldten's building and by the need to retain Lugovaia Street which connects Nevski Prospect with the square. Under these conditions, Rossi had no other choice but to duplicate the already existing curve with respect to the axis of symmetry of the Winter Palace on the other side of the square. To achieve the regularity called for by the then prevailing notions of symmetry it is hard to see how he could have chosen any other solution. Actually, another solution (preserved in the *Archive Meier*) had been advanced earlier but had been dismissed as extremely unsatisfactory. It proposed placing the complex of the General Staff in front of the buildings designed by Feldten. Had this project been executed, Dvortsovaia Square would have been virtually wiped out and the remaining open space would have merged with the narrow space of Admiralty Square.

The geometrical bisection of the curve which was obtained by duplicating the angle and curvature of the original half-section on the eastern side of the square thus became its clearly expressed axis of symmetry while at the same time defining the point of entry of Lugovaia Street. Sketches made by Rossi prove that he arrived at this solution very quickly and without hesitation. The only design variations deal with the form of the transition from Lugovaia Street into the space of the square and the architectural expression of the façades facing the Winter Palace. The general plan of the square as such was a logical extension of the ideas of Kvasov and Feldten, correctly interpreted and brought to their conclusion by Rossi (see illustration 32).

Dvortsovaia Square is quite different in shape and form from the other squares of the central city area. Among the rectangular spaces of the central ensemble it is distinguished by its individuality and unique shape. Thus Rossi's solution was a direct response to conditions which were exceptional and unique even before he began his work.

The spatial integration of Dvortsovaia Square, Admiralty Square next to it, and the other squares of the central ensemble is primarily a result of their adjacent location, their shape, and the general structural configuration of the overall plan. The curved recess of the General Staff Building—interrupting the general line of the buildings from St. Isaac Street to Pevcheski Bridge—is responsible for the individual character of the square and assures its partial spatial independence

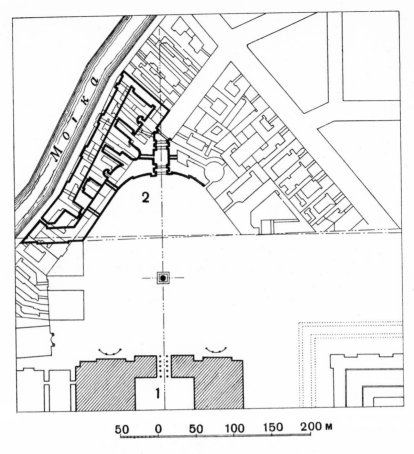

50   0   50   100   150   200 M

32. Final scheme for the reconstruction of Dvortsovaia Square.
1. Winter Palace; 2. General Staff Building.

within the overall system of the five squares of the central ensemble.

In contrast to the relatively effortless determination of the general layout, the design of the individual architectural features of the square proved to be much more difficult. Unfortunately very little material has been preserved tracing the complete sequence of Rossi's design. To begin with, there were no measured drawings of the building façades designed by Feldten. It is only known that Feldten entered a model in the

The reconstruction of Dvortsovaia Square

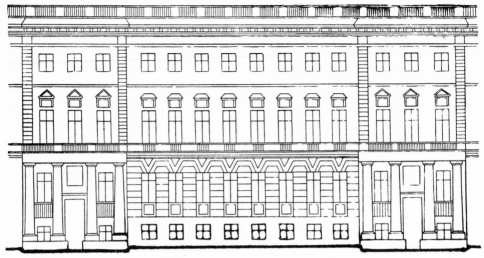

33. Dvortsovaia Square before reconstruction. Fragment of façade
of the building located on the south side of the square, designed
by Feldten.

previously mentioned competition. Quite obviously some
drawings must have been prepared for the actual construction. These or some other measured drawings were probably
used by Rossi for the planning of Dvortsovaia Square. So far
it has been impossible to find any of these, and therefore most
of the research concerning the reconstruction of the square
is based on a comparison of sketches and lithographs depicting the square before its reconstruction with its present appearance as well as on a number of other sketches to be
discussed later.

On the basis of some of the drawings showing the layout
of the square before reconstruction, it becomes evident that
the first attempts to achieve harmony between the façades of
the Winter Palace and the General Staff Building opposite
were already made by Feldten (see illustration 33). Feldten's
buildings were almost of the same height as the Winter Palace
opposite, the difference being so insignificant as to be virtually

imperceptible to the naked eye. Next he repeated the number of floors, the vertical articulation of the façade, and the horizontal bands of the cornice lines. Both the Winter Palace and Feldten's building opposite were divided horizontally into clearly defined upper and lower parts. Each of these consisted of two floors. The lower floors were in both cases united under a single heavy cornice and both buildings were crowned by a heavy parapet. The relative proportions of the lower to the upper floors in each building were also equal.

Thus the main elements establishing the architectural unity of the two facing complexes were: their similar height, an equal number of floors, similar vertical articulation, and the equal proportioning of their horizontal divisions. The last two items were of special importance for the future development of Rossi's design.

Comparing the architectural details of the two buildings, one can easily discover the following. In both the palace and the General Staff Building by Feldten the lower and upper windows are considerably smaller than the intermediate ones. Due to this the two lower floors can be taken for a single ground floor, whereas the upper two rows of windows give the impression of a double-lit space behind them. The similarity of the horizontal elements is further enhanced by the architectural resemblance of the two buildings. As a response to the porches and gates of the Winter Palace, Feldten placed four-column porticoes near the porches and gates of his building. Rastrelli had varied the design of the individual window details as well as the window frames. Following his example Feldten changed the design of the window details in the corresponding places of the façade of the General Staff Building. The general character of the architectural details was therefore similar in both buildings.

Apart from this apparent similarity of architectural detail

in Feldten's General Staff Building and the Winter Palace, there were certain fundamental differences. The palace was rectilinear, whereas the General Staff Building was of irregular shape. The plastic forms of the Winter Palace were enhanced by the numerous recesses and projections and the rich baroque details of its façade. In contrast, Feldten's building was quite different in its overall architectural conception. There were no projections or recesses, the details were much flatter, their outlines were crisp, and the façade had a sober, geometrical character. Thus, even before the reconstruction, elements of similarity as well as of disparity between the two buildings were evident.

Rossi did not arrive at the final design of the façade at once. His preliminary sketches have probably been lost, however, a number of drawings found in the Museum of the Academy of Arts gives some indication of the evolution of his design. His first design was obviously conceived under the influence of the close similarity between the two existing buildings (see illustration 34). In this early scheme Rossi attempted to reinforce even more the architectural verisimilitude between his project and the front elevation of the palace. He retained Feldten's four-column porticoes and, reflecting the projected central part of the palace, he attached a multicolumn portico to the central part of the façade, which in turn was pierced by three arches corresponding to the three arches of the entrance to the interior of the Winter Palace. However, it is difficult to judge the façade design of a building on the basis of a single floor plan. It is quite possible that the columns of the frontal porticoes were supposed to rise to the full height of the building as did the portico columns opposite, while it is equally possible that they were designed to cover the first two floors only. One thing is obvious—in terms of its plastic qualities and because of its close similarity to the opposite complex of the

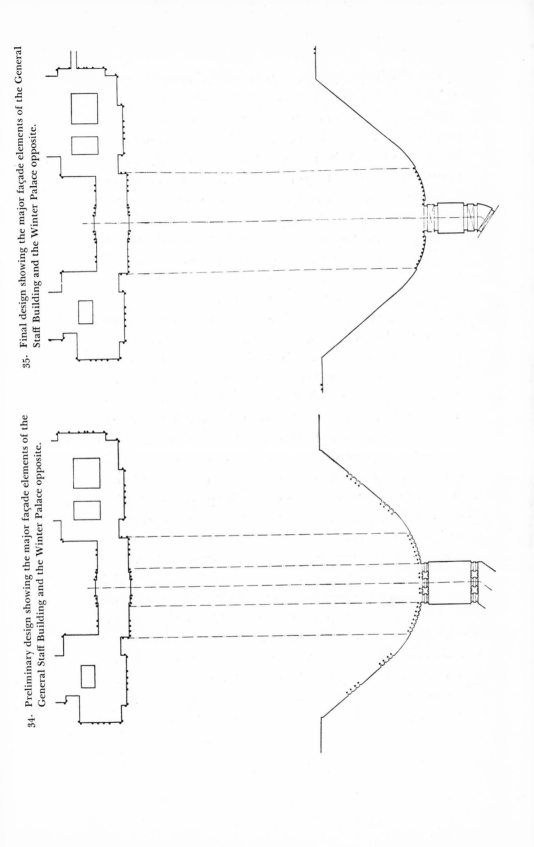

34. Preliminary design showing the major façade elements of the General Staff Building and the Winter Palace opposite.

35. Final design showing the major façade elements of the General Staff Building and the Winter Palace opposite.

Winter Palace, this scheme was in essence merely a further elaboration of Feldten's ideas.

However, a mere repetition of architectural details is not enough to achieve a truly unified architectural ensemble. The spatial location of the palace within the ensemble was predetermined by the general plan. The General Staff Building is located on the northern side of the square and thus receives full sunlight only during the short northern summer months. To compete with the plastic exuberance of Rastrelli's baroque details and the chiaroscuro play of light and dark on the southern sunbathed side of the square would be difficult under any circumstances and much more so by a mere repetition of architectural detail. Apart from these considerations, it was equally important to recognize the primacy of the square within the spatial structure of the whole ensemble. This could only be achieved by developing a design which would weaken the visual dominance of the palace over the space of the square. The solution of this problem was therefore really based on a paradox. On the one hand, the buildings had to be architecturally related to each other and the large space of the square between in a general way, while on the other hand the conditions of their spatial juxtaposition asked for both contrast and individuality, and an overall high level of architectural quality.

Rossi seems to have been aware of all these problems, and even though the few drawings which have been preserved do not sufficiently illustrate the complete sequence of the design process they nevertheless give a fair indication of the wide scope of his creative energy, proving at the same time that he was indeed not fully satisfied with the first scheme. His final scheme, which was eventually realized, takes into account all the conditions dictated by the character and the spatial configuration of the ensemble (see illustration 35). In this scheme

Rossi left the façade of Feldten's wing almost unchanged. He duplicated many of the elements on his side of the building, such as overall height, the proportion of the floors, the cornice lines, and a number of other architectural details. However, in contrast to the previous scheme he did not retain the four-column porticoes, and the entrances to the courtyards were designed without any ornament. He articulated the central part in order to accentuate its architectural relationship with respect to the central axis of the palace, and, as a consequence, its special significance as the most important spatial element in the structure of the general ensemble.

A careful study of the two opposite central elements reveals that the main porch of the Winter Palace and the central passage of the General Staff Building do indeed have much in common. One is equally struck by the subtle contrasts between them. In connection with this it should be pointed out that from no point within the square can they be simultaneously perceived.

The structural resemblance of the General Staff Building to the Winter Palace, discussed earlier in relation to Feldten's solution, was also maintained by Rossi and was further reinforced by some additional elements. The upper part of the building is unified by three-quarter columns, similar to those used by Rastrelli on the opposite side of the square. The central parts of both buildings are articulated separately. The central part of the Winter Palace was raised above the general height of the façade by means of a pediment bearing the imperial standard, while the corresponding counterpart of the General Staff Building was raised by means of an attic above the arch which, in turn, was topped by a sculptural group.

But literal similarity ends here, and Rossi's genius found its expression in the subtle way in which he was able to make the distinction between a mere copy of the existing details of the palace and an individual statement achieving overall unity within architectural diversity. Rastrelli's lines flow smoothly, effortlessly melting one into the other. Rossi's lines are clear and crisp. The individual parts of the palace display subtle nuances of recess and projection. Rossi's façade is tectonic and almost severe in character, the triumphal arch contrasting vividly with the rest of the elevation.

And here they stand, facing each other—Rastrelli's ornate baroque of the Winter Palace and the severe classicism of Rossi—showing the world an example of a remarkable ensemble, representing, in many ways, the best in the tradition of the classicist ideals of city building—namely the achievement of unity in variety.[6]

Rossi's final design was approved in 1819 and the expropriation of the properties on Dvortsovaia Square was begun. Construction was started during the following building season and continued until the year 1828. But all this was not yet sufficient to bring the space of Dvortsovaia Square to life. Even after the completion of the reconstruction works, the two major building masses acted as a mere architectural foil for the vast open space of the square and, in a manner of speaking, divided the space into two equal spheres of architectural influence. Something else was needed to fuse the two parts and to complete the design by means of a "final masterstroke." Moreover, Dvortsovaia Square needed to be integrated with the system of the other squares around the Admiralty Building.

In order to complete the task after the reconstruction of the south side, it was necessary to resolve its architectural termination at the eastern end. At the same time it was decided to place a monument in the center of the new square.

The need for a monument here was to a large degree dictated by the nature of the spatial structure of the five central squares. The spatial disposition of the ensemble not only called for the placement of an important monument but virtually dictated its exact location.

Dvortsovaia Square was part of the larger system of the five central squares, where each square merged into the next, and where each of the squares represented both an individual entity as well as part of a larger whole. Dvortsovaia Square represented the most important space of the whole ensemble, mainly because of the curved recess in its south side. However, this recess could not be seen from the other squares, such as Senate Square and Admiralty Square. Thus, its architectural termination and its spatial significance had to be articulated by other means. The monument provided the required element of visual concentration. The large parades of that period were held in the united space of all the five central squares. The troops usually took the route from St. Isaac Cathedral toward Dvortsovaia Square, where the parade would terminate. Thus the monument would be visible from the distance, clearly marking the goal for the moving columns of parading soldiers.

There was another reason for the placement of a tall monument in Dvortsovaia Square. During the construction of the General Staff Building, all the existing buildings on the eastern side of the square were demolished with the single exception of the drill hall at its eastern end. As a result, the buildings on the opposite shore of the Moika visually entered the space of the square. These buildings, spread along the shore of the Moika, were not designed to be included in the spatial structure of the ensemble of the central squares and were therefore not suitable as an architectural terminus for the eastern end of the square. The monument was thus able to fulfill another important function. It became a visual point of concentration, for as one looked from the Riding Academy toward Dvortsovaia Square, it effectively masked the imperfection of the view behind the Moika. All of these considerations clearly pointed to the need for a monument. The question of its exact location within the square was more difficult. Here too the spatial structure of the ensemble helped to predetermine the exact spot for its location in Dvortsovaia Square.

Obviously one of the coordinates had to coincide with the axis of symmetry of Dvortsovaia Square. This was dictated by the architecture of the square and the axial location of the central archway of the General Staff Building. Any deviation from this strong axis of symmetry would not have been permissible. Given the artistic tastes of this period, and owing to the axial character of most of the classicist compositions, a deviation from the axis of symmetry would have been hard to imagine. Thus, the first coordinate was irrefutably fixed to coincide with the main axis of Dvortsovaia Square.

The other coordinate was more difficult to determine. Pencil lines superimposed on one of the general plans of Dvortsovaia Square indicate a number of possible locations for the proposed monument—the Alexander Column.[7] It is not certain whether these markings were made by Rossi or by Montferrand, but whoever made them was certainly giving serious thought to the correct location of the monument (see illustration 36). One point, determined by the intersection of line D–D and the axis of symmetry A–A, places the monument at the geometrical center of the arch formed by the building of the General Staff. It seems that only a masterful designer such as Rossi could have indicated this particular location. Its choice took into consideration the view from the windows of the Winter Palace. Only from there would the column have

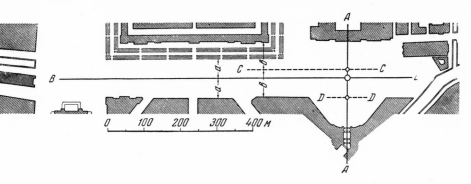

36. Design analysis of the possible locations of the Alexander Column in the space of Dvortsovaia Square.

appeared to be in the visual center of the open space of the square. However, in relation to the rest of the ensemble such a location for the Alexander Column would have been an unsatisfactory solution. An alternate location was indicated by the intersection of the axis of symmetry A–A and the co-ordinate C–C, which marked the center line between the façade of the Admiralty and the opposite façade of the General Staff complex. This seemed to be the most logical solution, but it failed to take into account some of the more subtle relationships of the ensemble. The space in front of the Admiralty was not really a single, unified space, since part of it was occupied by Admiralty Boulevard. Viewed along the perspective from the Riding Academy toward Dvortsovaia Square a column in the geometrical center between the buildings facing each other across the square would have appeared awkward and arbitrary.

As mentioned before, the outer limit of Admiralty Boulevard was determined by the "adjustment" of the axis of the Riding Academy with respect to the axis of Admiralty Square. In the search for the correct location of the Alexander Column this concept was recognized and developed to its logical conclusion. The coordinate B–B was placed in the geometrical center between the outer boundary of Admiralty Boulevard and the opposite façades of Admiralty Square (see illustration 36).

Fixed by the intersection of coordinates A–A and B–B, the location of the monument was correct both with respect to the interior spatial organization of Dvortsovaia Square as well as in relation to the overall system of the larger central ensemble. It underlined the central axis of Dvortsovaia Square and thus, in turn, the axial symmetry of the main building complexes on each of its opposite sides (see illustration 37). In addition, it exerted a strong visual pull for anyone approaching the ensemble via the central arch of the General Staff passage. Within the general space of the five central squares it, as it were, covered up the distant view behind the Moika, and during military parades it provided a visual goal for the marching troops. Thus, the Alexander Column emphasized the spatial significance of Dvortsovaia Square and, in addition, helped to fix the visual center of Admiralty Boulevard by providing a counterpoint to the centrally located entrance of the Riding Academy. (See illustration 43.)

This point, determined by the intersection of coordinates A–A and B–B, was ultimately selected as the actual location of the Alexander Column. The so-called "Pedestal for Alexander" thus became an organic part of the spatial structure of the central squares and an integral element of the general architectural organization of the ensemble. It is fortunate that the design of the monument itself is rather static. It would have been very difficult to place a work of dynamic character in the space of Dvortsovaia Square. It is also very fortunate that it was conceived as a vertical element. Thus it neither interfered with the movement of the parading troops nor obstructed the view toward the eastern part of the ensemble. The vertical fitted well into the general architectural picture,

37. Elevational drawing of the façade of the General Staff Building
with the triumphal arch in the center and the Alexander Column
in front on the same scale.

being most effective—as it still is—when seen from the archway of the General Staff Building. Finally, the verticality of
the column provided a striking contrast to the generally horizontal character of the surrounding buildings.

The choice of material for the column was also successful.
It was similar to that used in the construction of St. Isaac
Cathedral and therefore provided a necessary architectural

link between the latter and Dvortsovaia Square. Had this not been done, the cathedral would have been completely different both in material and color from the rest of the buildings surrounding the five central squares. The design of the column was less successful. Its motif was based on a number of existing prototypes in Europe and could certainly not be considered an original piece of work.

The principal merits of the Alexander Column are its location and its spatial relationship to the rest of the ensemble. The uniqueness of the square was certainly not due to the introduction of Montferrand's monument. But the spatial ties between Dvortsovaia Square and the other squares of the ensemble were indubitably much strengthened by the introduction of the "Pedestal of Alexander."

The last project in the area of Dvortsovaia Square was the construction of the Staff Building of the Royal Guard Regiments by A. Briullov in 1840. Some years before, during the erection of the Alexander Column in 1827, Rossi had proposed two alternative schemes for the architectural termination of the east side of the square. One would assume that being the main participant in the reconstruction of Dvortsovaia Square, Rossi would have subordinated the architectural appearance of his proposed scheme for the east side of the square to the character of the surrounding buildings. This view is wrong, however, for Rossi's design cannot be judged solely on the basis of its limited context within the confines of Dvortsovaia Square. Judged on the basis of such a limited point of view the building would certainly have appeared alien and unrelated to the Winter Palace and the General Staff complex. Only within the total system of the ensemble does the true aim of his design proposals become comprehensible. By recognizing the visual implications of the vast open space which extended almost 1,000 meters from the proposed Staff Building of the Royal Guard Regiments toward the west, Rossi achieved a valid solution to the problem of the spatial unification of Dvortsovaia Square and the rest of the ensemble of the central squares.

In the two proposed schemes for the east side of the square, Rossi made the elevation of the Staff Building of the Royal Guards similar to that of Quarenghi's Riding Academy. In the first solution he placed the axis of the central portico in line with the outer edge of Admiralty Boulevard. This solution was rejected as unsatisfactory. The second solution shows twin porticoes, one closing the perspective from the boulevard, the other one completing the square toward the north. One can easily imagine that the implementation of the latter scheme would have provided a definite architectural termination to the system of the central squares, anchoring Dvortsovaia Square even more securely to the spatial structure of the central ensemble. This would have produced a spatial tension between the unique character of the square and its integration with the rest of the ensemble without destroying the overall architectural unity of the five central squares.

When Briullov took over the design of the Staff Building of the Royal Guard Regiments, the Alexander Column was already in place. This effectively changed the character of the environment into which the new building was to be placed. As a result of its careful siting the monument functioned quite successfully as the unifying element between the square and the other spaces of the central ensemble. Only in the light of these facts can one understand why Briullov considered as primary the architectural relationship between the new building and the palace on one side and that of the General Staff on the other side, and why he chose to ignore the original aim of Rossi's plan conceived some thirteen years earlier.

The Staff Building of the Royal Guard Regiments was the

last project in the reconstruction of Dvortsovaia Square. It became the architectural link between the buildings of different periods, such as the Hermitage and the Zapasni Palace, and represented the transition between the works of such masters as de la Mothe and Feldten. It is to Briullov's credit that he was sensitive enough to respect the spatial importance of the existing Alexander Column and that he did not express the axis of symmetry in his design, which would have weakened the spatial significance of both.

However, he failed to grasp the importance of his project as part of the larger complex of all the five central squares and so did not provide additional architectural links to strengthen the spatial ties between the building and the rest of the ensemble. He did not see that the general expression of Dvortsovaia Square was to a large degree based on architectural contrasts, a fact well understood by Rossi in his brilliant solution for the General Staff Building. This building was successful not because of a literal verisimilitude with the Winter Palace but, quite to the contrary, because of the many architectural contrasts between it and the palace.

After its reconstruction Dvortsovaia Square became one of the most important spaces of the city center. This was due mainly to its location near the Winter Palace and the high architectural quality of all its component elements. Its spatial unity was accomplished by the architectural juxtaposition of the Winter Palace and the General Staff Building, by its peculiar shape, and by its spatial, architectural, and visual ties with the other squares. Its successful integration into the urban fabric of the whole central area of the city was achieved by virtue of all these factors which, in aggregate, represented the principal qualities of the ensemble.

8

The reconstruction of Senate Square and St. Isaac Square

The next major project in the central part of St. Petersburg during the first half of the 19th century was the reconstruction of Senate Square, now called Dekabrist (Decembrist) Square.

At present the square is a self-contained space. Alexander Park, established between 1872 and 1874, occupies all of the area of the former Admiralty Square, including a considerable part of the former Senate Square. The large trees of the park now divide the former unified space of the ensemble of the five central squares into separate parts. However, in the first half of the 19th century, Senate Square was still an organic part of the large space of the central squares.

Three major complexes define the architectural limits of Senate Square: the Admiralty, St. Isaac Cathedral, and the united buildings of the Senate and the Holy Synod. The most important architectural element within the space of both Senate Square and St. Isaac Square is the large complex of St. Isaac Cathedral. The cathedral is the only building whose spatial sphere of influence is not confined to the area of the central squares. Its importance as a major architectural element within the overall system of the central squares, as well as within the general skyline of the city, was well understood by the designers of that period.

After the end of the Napoleonic wars it was proposed to provide the city of St. Petersburg with a large structure which would dominate the rest of its building masses and which would mark its architectural center even when viewed from a great distance. Based on the example of other large capital cities of the time such a landmark could hardly be anything else but the dome of a large cathedral, surpassing in size all the other cupolas of the city. The need for its reconstruction was rationalized by the claim that the time had come to "give a decent appearance" to old St. Isaac Cathedral.

The old cathedral had been built in great haste and with many major departures from the original design by Antonio Rinaldi. After the completion of the other reconstruction projects in this area of the city the old cathedral stood out in poor contrast to the new buildings surrounding it. In 1815 it was definitely decided to rebuild St. Isaac Cathedral. A competition was held with most of the important architects of the capital submitting entries. But the competition had no influence on the final design of the new cathedral since none of the entries was accepted. The sequence of events leading to the selection of a design for the cathedral is rather confused. This confusion is further compounded by statements published by Montferrand [1] in a monograph dealing with the design of the cathedral. [2] There is also some reason to believe that Montferrand knowingly added to the ensuing confusion by the publication of another monograph which attempted to explain the design of the cathedral in even greater detail.

Montferrand arrived in St. Petersburg from his native France in 1816, apparently not without some previous solicitations on his behalf by his patron Betancourt, who was at that time the chairman of the Committee for Construction and Hydraulic Works. Soon after his arrival Montferrand was asked to prepare plans for the reconstruction of St. Isaac Cathedral with the stipulation that as much as possible of the existing structure was to be preserved. Montferrand subsequently drew up approximately twenty small sketch-designs, more or less in accordance with the dimensions of the old cathedral. On the basis of these sketches he was appointed court architect.

On February 20, 1818, one of these preliminary designs was approved. A Building Commission for the Reconstruction of St. Isaac Square was established, with Betancourt at its head. During the year 1818 the necessary building materials were purchased and brought to the site, and by the following year the first foundation piles were driven.

The approval of Montferrand's project and the commencement of the reconstruction work provoked great agitation in the architectural circles of St. Petersburg. It seemed incomprehensible to all the architects of the capital that a comparatively unknown newcomer who had not distinguished himself by any previous significant work should be given the biggest and most important commission in the city. The project was much discussed in the city's professional circles and opinions differed widely as to whether St. Isaac Cathedral would become for St. Petersburg what St. Peter's had become for Rome, or St. Paul's for London, or Brunelleschi's Duomo for Florence.

In 1820 Montferrand made a tactical error by publishing his first book about the cathedral including his drawings of the project.[3] Although this almost prevented Montferrand from completing the cathedral, the publication of his design had fortunate consequences for the future of the St. Petersburg center. Up to this point the architects and artists of the capital had known little about Montferrand's actual intentions and much of what they did know was based on conjecture and guesswork. After the publication of the book, the design, and thus the future appearance of the cathedral, became public property.

The axial relationships of the cathedral to the square were the first items to provoke criticism. According to Montferrand's drawings the axis of symmetry of the cathedral porticoes passed through the center between the Senate Building and the outer boundary of Admiralty Boulevard. Prof. A. Melnikov, attacking this concept wrote:

> . . . the cathedral should be placed in the geometrical center of the square, which is defined by the line midway between the opposite façades of the Admiralty and the Senate. The failure to do so will certainly be regretted in the future, as the cathedral will lose its apparent size in perspective. The center line between the façade of the Senate and the outer limit of Admiralty Boulevard cannot be regarded as the center line of the square, since there are clear spaces between the trees while these, in turn, are much lower in height than the Admiralty.[4]

Given the large size of Senate Square it really made little difference whether Montferrand's design or Melnikov's solution was adopted. In fairness to Montferrand it must be said that his solution had greater merit, mainly because the central axes of the other two squares around the Admiralty—Admiralty Square and Razvodnaia Square—also passed midway between the façades on one side and the other edge of Admiralty Boulevard on the other side, thus consistently tying the separate squares into one single ensemble.

During a meeting of the architectural members of the Academy held in the Academy of Arts on October 21, 1820, and on the basis of a request by the architect Modiui, who was on the staff of the Committee of Construction and Hydraulic Works, a motion was introduced severely criticizing both the design of St. Isaac Cathedral and the manner in which the work was being executed on the site. The participants resolved that the "subject matter of this motion is of such grave importance that it warrants most diligent scrutiny and careful investigation." [5] It was also proposed to "hear the opinions of the other side, in order to compare the two positions." [6]

After imperial consent had been secured, a committee was appointed and invested with the task of investigating Modiui's charges. It was composed of professors and members of the Academy of Arts, as well as of the architects Rossi, Bazen, and de Strem.

As expressed by the president of the Academy, A. Olenin, the attitude of the committee toward the two protagonists—Montferrand and Modiui—was rather interesting. Olenin wrote:

> One may well say that either of these two gentlemen can speak about the work in question only in terms of conjecture, since both have to admit in all honesty that they have little actual experience in these matters, for the simple reason that building projects on such a large scale are very rare indeed at the present time, either in France or in any other foreign country.[7]

Soon after receiving Montferrand's reply the committee entered upon a detailed examination of the various remarks, observations, arguments and counter-arguments, including the on-site study of the project itself. These deliberations continued until the end of 1822, in effect, for almost a full year. During this period all construction was stopped.

The essence of Modiui's complaint was his contention that it was practically impossible to build the cathedral according to Montferrand's plans. Three reasons were given to support this claim: Modiui charged that it was impossible to support the new dome partially on old and partially on new foundations, arguing that the ensuing differential settlement would eventually threaten the whole structure with collapse. Secondly, even if the foundations held, the dome could not be built, owing to the fact that, in Montferrand's design, the lateral loads were not properly distributed. Thirdly, Modiui claimed that Montferrand was incapable of undertaking a work of such magnitude for the simple reason that on the evidence of his plans he simply did not know how to build.

In its final conclusions the committee agreed in general with Modiui's criticism, ruling that it was:

> . . . impossible to carry out the reconstruction of the cathedral according to the plans submitted by Montferrand . . . more time, money and effort will be required to bring such an important project to its proper conclusion. . . .
>
> Having expressed its opinion concerning the lack of structural stability of Montferrand's project the committee furthermore considers it as its duty to . . . state its opinion concerning the design itself. Faced with the problem of having to retain as much of the existing structure of the cathedral as possible, Montferrand seems to have been unable to find any better solution for the dome than to design it in such a way that the space circumscribed by the cupola is larger than the space below. . . . The drawings show clearly . . . first, that the lower space below the dome is much narrower

than the upper one . . . and secondly, that St. Isaac Cathedral, despite its considerable external dimensions would appear small from the interior, mainly because of the close proximity of the columns which divide the interior of the cathedral into numerous small spaces, thus making it impossible to obtain a complete view of the whole interior, which, in addition, is cluttered up with numerous other objects . . . thirdly and finally, due to this fragmented layout, and also owing to the fact that the lower part of the cathedral is provided with only very few windows the interior would be dark and almost devoid of daylight. . . .

. . . having discovered these serious deficiencies, the commission feels compelled to conclude . . . that these faults should be eliminated, and that the cathedral should be redesigned in such a manner that both its interior and exterior relate to each other in general size and scale, and in accordance with the magnificence and monumentality of such an important complex. . . .[8]

Considerable time went by and finally, in February, 1824, an ukase was issued settling the cathedral's destiny.[9] Montferrand's original project was rejected, and the committee had to decide whether the existing plans should be completely reworked or a new design called for. The majority of the members of the committee, many of whom were men of considerable talent, had little experience in matters of collective design and were at that time preoccupied with their own projects. These and other factors held up the further development of St. Isaac Cathedral, while little was done to bring the project to successful completion.

Soon thereafter Rossi left the commission, being at this time fully occupied with other projects, including the reconstruction of Dvortsovaia Square. Starov also was unable to give the matter his full attention. As a result the committee was deprived of the services of its most talented members—Starov and Rossi—who would have been the most capable of suggesting a counter-proposal of sufficient quality to defeat Montferrand's scheme.

During two consecutive sessions on June 3, and 4, 1824, the committee examined and appraised projects submitted by Starov, Mikhailov I, Mikhailov II, Beretti, and Melnikov. On June 19, 1824, the committee selected the best project by secret ballot. In this highly original competition, where the participants and the jury were the same, the final votes were distributed in the following manner: the project of Academy Rector Mikhailov I—21 points; the project of Academy Member Mikhailov II—14 points; the project of Academy Member Starov—9 points; the project of Academy Member Beretti— also 9 points; and the project of Professor Melnikov—3 points.

While the members of the committee occupied their time by arranging private competitions, Montferrand used his to prepare a new design, carefully taking into consideration all the criticism leveled against his first scheme by Modiui and the conditions outlined by the ukase of Alexander I.

> . . . when all the projects were presented . . . to His Royal Highness—His Majesty was particularly pleased with the project of the elder Mikhailov, but not withstanding this the new, corrected project of Montferrand was later approved for actual construction and the works now in progress were carried out in accordance with these plans.[10]

Montferrand's new project had little in common with his previous one. Being a brilliant adapter of other peoples' ideas, he combined the best features of all the other proposals and at the same time managed to retain those parts of the old cathedral that Alexander I wanted to preserve. To begin with, he held to the rectangular shape of the cathedral, though most of the other architects had changed it to a square, a form which is unquestionably more suitable to the static form of the traditional Russian five-cupola church. However, while keeping the rectangular plan, Montferrand succeeded in correcting it by moving the smaller cupolas closer to the main dome. In order to achieve this, he had to introduce small projections in the plan below these smaller cupolas. The main dome was placed on completely new foundations, and all the structural omissions which had been criticized in the first project were duly corrected. Finally, the relationship between the large dome and the four side cupolas was changed considerably. In the old project their scale relationship was lifeless and dull; in the new one the large dome clearly dominated the others.

Still, much was left to be done by other architects and artists to complete this final project. A great deal was changed, very often for the better, before the huge mass of the cathedral finally rose over St. Petersburg. This detailed account of the course of events accompanying the reconstruction of St. Isaac Cathedral is necessary not only for an evaluation of Montferrand's contribution to the design of St. Isaac's Cathedral and for further analysis of the ensemble of squares, but it is equally necessary for a full understanding of the way in which large projects were commissioned and approved during that period. Moreover, it reveals the causes of the mistakes made in the design of the cathedral which was to become the architectural dominant of the city.

In relation to the general ensemble the designers had to solve two major problems: the organic integration of the cathedral complex with the spatial structure of the central squares; and the role of this structure as the dominant architectural element in the skyline of the whole city. Both these requirements were to a considerable degree in conflict with each other. The integration of the cathedral into the structural fabric of the central squares required the coordination of its architectural elements, massing, materials, and colors, with the existing buildings and those under construction in its vicinity. At the same time its role as an architectural dominant required a change of scale by an increase in the size of its individual parts. Viewed out of the context of the cathedral's immediate surroundings, these contrasts are hardly noticeable. The huge dome crowning the edifice helps to mask many of the scale discrepancies between the cathedral and the adjacent buildings. It is obvious that Montferrand did not solve the first task very satisfactorily, or perhaps he ignored it. Quite aside from the lack of architectural unity between St. Isaac Cathedral and the Admiralty and Senate opposite, Montferrand did nothing to achieve architectural harmony between the cathedral and the adjacent house of Lobanov-Rostovski which he had also designed. Their scale discrepancies are obvious and it must be assumed that Montferrand did not attempt to integrate either of them with the general ensemble. The cathedral rises like a solitary gray mass among the architecturally disciplined and unified projects of Zakharov, Rossi, and Quarenghi.

The second task, the definition of the architectural center of the city from the views opening up beyond and around it and the strengthening of the spatial dominance of the main ensemble in the silhouette of the city, was successfully achieved by the mass and shape of the large dome of the cathedral. However, this was accomplished not only because the dome was "visible from a distance of 40 versts" as Montferrand wrote (although such prominence in terms of size was certainly a basic requirement) but also through the designer's felicitous choice of suitable proportions for the individual parts of the dome and their correct distribution. From the far distance, from the shores of Vasilevski Island, from the Vyborg District, and even from the Gulf of Finland, the outline of the main bulk of the cathedral rises elegantly above the surrounding buildings. The penetration of the lower building masses by the dome is accomplished gradually rather than by brutal disruption. Similarly, looked at from a distance, the various joints between the porticoes and the roof are hidden by the surrounding buildings. The relationship between the combined masses of the supporting drum and the dome and the four surrounding cupolas is also quite successful.

In his reworked scheme Montferrand paid attention to the commission's criticism of the position of the four cupolas surrounding the main dome and moved them toward the center, describing the corners of a perfect square. This corrected a serious architectural mistake which would have been immediately apparent within the general structure of the central ensemble. Due to the square layout of the side cupolas, the form of the cathedral appears static from a distance, which is essential to its function as the central architectural landmark of the city.

One may therefore react to this "semicollective design" in two ways. On the one hand, it is necessary to state that, within the ensemble of the squares and within the spatial context of Senate Square, the cathedral was out of scale, but that this was not due to its absolute size. Had Montferrand studied the scale relationships of the Smolny Monastery Cathedral, he could have learned from this example how to achieve the transition from the large scale of the dome to that of the four subsidiary cupolas and, finally, to the detail scale of the surrounding buildings. Unfortunately Montferrand knew only how to compile and copy, lacking a full understanding of the many lessons and implications furnished by the existing architectural heritage of the city. Because of various circumstances the other designers of that period were able to help only indirectly.

On the other hand, having said all this, one must admit that the addition of St. Isaac Cathedral to the St. Petersburg skyline provided a badly needed "crown" for the center of the city. The dome became the final, albeit not the most ideal, element in the spatial structure of the city center. It defined the architectural center of St. Petersburg and provided the terminal element for many important vistas which would otherwise have remained incomplete.

Two years after the approval of the final cathedral design, the question of the reconstruction of the western side of Senate Square was raised. On August 10, 1827, after inspecting the building of the Senate, Nikolai I gave instructions for its immediate reconstruction on the model of the General Staff Building. The mention of the General Staff Building as an example is not without interest. It indicates that this project had gained approval not only from professionals but also from the other members of the elite. Architect Staubert was asked to submit a design but his project was not approved. After that, another competition was held. The ground rules of the competition made it clear that first consideration was to be given to the ensemble and that "the building of the Senate should be designed in such a manner as to be in harmony with the large size of the square on which it is located." [11] The competition closed in February, 1829. From the many schemes which were submitted Rossi's project was selected as the winning entry and was later approved without any major modifications. The construction of the building was supervised by Staubert. It must be mentioned that the project of the Senate and Synod complex was carried out under special circumstances which greatly influenced the architectural design of the two buildings.

At first, only the reconstruction of the Senate Building, which occupied part of the western side of the square, was proposed. The reconstruction of this building alone would have left the ensemble of the square incomplete. Rossi proposed to rebuild the full width of the western side of the square from the waterfront to the Riding Academy, suggesting a unified façade along the whole length. However, the program called only for the reconstruction of the Senate portion of the building. This meant that only this part of the project had the assurance of realization.

It was therefore necessary to proceed on the assumption that the realization of the other half of the scheme—the future Synod Building—would be postponed or abandoned altogether. In consequence, both possibilities had to be considered. The west side of the square had to be designed as an architectural unit and also as part of the overall ensemble of the square. Moreover, Rossi had to provide for the possibility that after the Senate had been rebuilt and given architectural integrity and independence, permission would be granted for the completion of the other half of the scheme— the addition of the Synod Building—which would then have to become part of a unified whole.

In response to these conditions Rossi prepared two solutions for the competition: one for the reconstruction of only the Senate Building in its existing location and another showing its unification with the future Synod Building on the site then occupied by the house of someone named Kuzovnikov.[12] The second solution, which unified the two buildings by means of a central archway, was approved and soon after the Holy Synod became the client for the second half of the project.

Apart from the difficulties connected with the conditions of the program, Rossi was faced by problems stemming from the location of the buildings within the structure of the central ensemble of St. Petersburg and their spatial disposi-

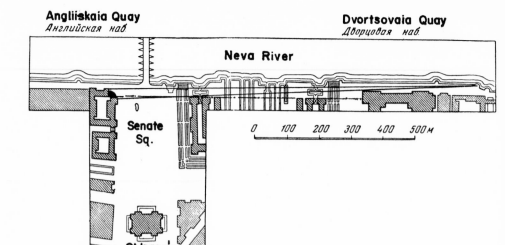

38. Plan of Senate Square in the middle of the 19th century.

tion within the system of Senate Square itself. The spatial significance of the project within the system of the square is therefore of vital importance.

After the sidewings of the Admiralty had been pulled back from the Neva toward the interior, the projecting corners of the Winter Palace and the building on the English Quay opposite became quite important architecturally. The recessing of the Admiralty wings opened the perspective between Dvortsovaia Quay and Angliiskaia Quay. The view along the quays was now terminated by the end projections of the Senate and the Admiralty respectively. As a result these two opposite corners became important elements not only in the design of Senate Square but equally so in terms of their juxtaposition within the general space of the central ensemble (see illustration 38).

The Winter Palace, the General Staff Building, the War Ministry, St. Isaac Cathedral, in short, all the buildings around the Admiralty, both existing and under construction, were higher than the complex at the center. Looking toward the central ensemble across the Neva or from a distance, one had the impression that the Admiralty had gradually been surrounded by a "frame" of higher buildings. In order to complete the balance of the ensemble it was necessary to increase the overall height of the Senate and Synod complex.

Factors other than height also had to be considered. The visual relationship between the Senate and Synod complex and the Winter Palace within the ensemble around the Admiralty Building and the open perspective along the quays were also important. The architectural character of the Winter Palace—strange though this may seem at first glance—therefore exerted great influence on the design of the Senate and Synod. Let us therefore examine how the position of the Senate and Synod complex within the system of Senate Square and opposite the completed façade of the sidewing of the Admiralty affected Rossi's design.

The main axis of Senate Square was obviously determined by the central axes of St. Isaac Cathedral and that of the pontoon bridge across the Neva on its opposite side. Due to its large mass and its location, the cathedral was clearly the main architectural element among all the other buildings surrounding the square. In order to balance the composition, the western part of the square had to correspond in general character and architectural expression to the eastern side. In other words, the façade of the Senate and Synod had to be related to the façade of the Admiralty Building. The secondary axis of the square was determined by the axis of symmetry of the Admiralty sidewing elevation and thus had to be recognized in the design of the new Senate and Synod complex. Furthermore, the very presence of the large bulk of St. Isaac Cathedral suggested a symmetrical solution of the lateral sides of the square which in turn called for the integration of the stylistic character and the compositional structure of the Senate and Synod with those of the Admiralty façade.

Thus the ensemble required the creation of a unified elevation along the full length of the west side of Senate Square, whereas the functional requirements called for a separate design for the façade of the Senate, independent and complete in itself. The spatial structure of Senate Square demanded the balance of its side elevations while the view from the opposite shore called for one elevation to be higher than the other. The location of the Senate and Synod within the spatial structure of Senate Square asked for a massing with a clearly expressed central axis. Similarly, the architectural treatment of the façade of the Admiralty wing and the closing of the perspective along the quays demanded the articulation of the projecting part near the waterfront.

In order to achieve architectural unity within the area of the square itself an expression sympathetic to the sober Doric of the Admiralty had to be found, while the view of the ensemble from the outside confirmed the necessity of relating the design to the architecture and style of the Winter Palace. However, that was not all. The main axis of Galernaia Street, separating the Senate from the Synod, was not parallel to the central longitudinal axis of the Admiralty, which introduced an additional element of spatial disharmony to be resolved by Rossi.

The recognition of the complexity of this tangle of contradictions was actually a relatively simple part of the task in comparison with the difficulties connected with arriving at a correct architectural solution. Only a brilliant designer like Rossi was equal to this task. The well-known projects of the other competitors—Staubert, Stasov, Giaco, and others—cannot bear comparison with his design, even if one were to judge

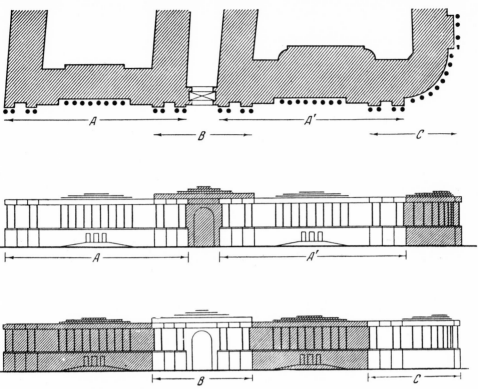

39. Schematic plan and elevations of the Senate and Synod complex
on the west side of Senate Square.

them solely on the strength of their solution of the architectural relationships within the ensemble.

In order to achieve a unified composition of the Senate and
Synod buildings while at the same time preserving their
architectural independence, Rossi proceeded as follows: Galernaia Street enters the square near its central axis, dividing
the project into two almost equal parts. Rossi treated each of
the two elevations as equal but independent entities, each
symmetrical within itself. Their main architectural features
were loggias and projecting porticoes with two columns each.
Thus, if only the Senate had been built, as originally planned,
it would have represented an architectural whole, independent and complete in itself (see illustration 39).

The part of the Senate marked "C" on the sketch represents the extent of its projection beyond the end of the side-wing of the Admiralty. In its design Rossi solved the problem of closing the perspective along Dvortsovaia Quay. Before the reconstruction, the corner of the existing building was not rounded, and Rossi's solution required considerable demolition of the existing structure and was quite costly. Obviously he was convinced that the additional expense incurred by this change was warranted by the results.

The rounded corner (C), starting where the Admiralty wing would end if projected across the square, made it possible to solve some of the contradictions within the ensemble in one single stroke. Above all, such a solution made it possible to design the rest of the elevations of the Senate and the Synod in such a way as to be in harmony with the architectural composition of the sidewing of the Admiralty. Due to its round form, the corner differed from the rest of the elevation, which was linear in character, and thus escaped the direct architectural influence of the Admiralty. It was therefore possible to design the rounded corner of the building without affecting the interrelationships between the opposite sides of the square with the added advantage that such a solution provided the desired visual terminus of the view along Dvortsovaia Quay toward the west. The rounded end part also helped to equalize the two separate elevations with respect to the center line of Galernaia Street and the axis of the Square, which in turn made it easier to unite the two identical compositions into one whole by means of a central arch.

A careful analysis reveals four distinct elevational elements: 1. the separate elevations of the Senate (A') and the Synod (A); 2. the rounded portion of the corner (C); 3. the arch between the two buildings (B); 4. the overall elevation as a unified whole. The composition of the central arch was strengthened by the façade elements of both the Senate and the Synod, namely, the two-column porticoes and the covering frieze. In order to accentuate the central axis the arch was crowned by an attic and a sculptural group. Thus the arch can be read as a separate compositional element as well as an integral part of the whole. Similarly, the two porticoes flanking the arch can be seen as an integral part of the central composition as well as architectural elements belonging to each of the two elevations to the right and left of the central arch.

Rossi used the two-column porticoes to tie the two separate parts into a unified whole. The porticoes not only define the end of one building but also accomplish the transition via the archway to the other one. In addition to all this they also act as a distinct link (B) between the two adjacent structures.

By such devices Rossi achieved unity in diversity and managed to overcome the many difficulties posed by the program. The fluidity of one element merging into the other betrays certain baroque tendencies in this example of Rossi's work. It is also possible that this was a subtle response to the influence of the Winter Palace, which was thus drawn into the design not so much by a repetition of its architectural details as by the organization of the general character of the composition. Some of these compositional elements are: the corner, the arch, the Senate and the Synod buildings as a unified complex and then again as separate entities. They were separate in the sense that each of them built individually would still represent a complete architectural statement, and they were unified in the sense that the designer was faced with the task of their eventual integration. And finally, they were part of the whole in the sense that the two-column porticoes are elements of two separate design motifs while at the same time accomplishing their unification.

One may now proceed to ask how architectural unity was achieved between the Senate and Synod complex and the façade of the sidewing of the Admiralty. If we compare the two structures the following similarities can be noticed: their common yellow-white color, the abundance of sculptural-decorative ornamentation, and the three-part articulation of the façades. However, there are also elements of contrast. Each building is based on a classical style of a different period. The calm dignity of Zakharov's Doric is brought into sharp contrast with the plastic play of Rossi's lively façade, the intricacy of its composition and the stateliness of the Corinthian order of the columns.

The use of a single style or the simple repetition of similar elements of style or plastic expression does not in itself guarantee architectural unity. On the contrary, such unity is often achieved by the use of many contrasting elements carefully juxtaposed. Dvortsovaia Square is a striking example of this concept. The buildings of the Senate and the Synod are seven feet higher than the sidewings of the Admiralty. From the square itself, this is hardly noticeable; however, from the other side of the Neva this difference in height can be readily discerned, thus proving the soundness of Rossi's solution. If the height had been the same as that of the Admiralty, the architectural and spatial balance of the central ensemble would have been upset.

The fact that Rossi decided to integrate the design of the Senate and Synod with the general spatial structure of the whole central ensemble considerably complicated the task of achieving architectural unity between the two opposite façades of Senate Square itself. In addition to the already noted similarity of individual architectural details, unity between the opposite façades was further reinforced by the use of similar designs. There is a definite resemblance between the façade of the Admiralty wing and that of the Senate and Synod in the articulation of their architectural masses. The main elements of the Admiralty façade are its three porticoes. These are echoed by Rossi's two-column porticoes on the opposite side of the square. In both elevations the main accent is on the center, which is articulated by a gable in one case and by an attic in the other. Finally, the structural fabric of the two complexes also reveals many similar features, such as the spacing of the vertical elements and the general treatment of the horizontal masses. In both cases the first floor is rusticated and serves as a base for the upper floors, which are unified by pilasters and columns.

All these factors, i.e., the recognition of the main axis of symmetry, the juxtaposition of architectural details, the similarity of the structural system, the control of floor heights and the use of one overall color scheme, add to the singular unity and the spatial balance of the two opposite sides of Senate Square. Notwithstanding all these common features, both compositions still retain their individuality. Certainly the mere repetition of the Admiralty façade on the other side of the Senate Square could never have been considered an ideal solution. Rossi's design of the Senate and Synod complex bears witness to his thorough analysis and understanding of all the problems involved; and his brilliant solution proves his ability to deal with them successfully. But even though all the complex tasks imposed by the conditions of the site and the nature of the ensemble were so masterfully accomplished, vicious attempts were made to undermine the master's reputation. Many of his contemporaries, criticizing the complex out of context of the many conditions and limitations so well understood by Rossi, spread stories about a decline in his creative powers—the same Rossi, who, while directing the reconstruction of the Senate and Synod complex was simultaneously creating his greatest masterpiece, the ensemble of the Alexander Theater. Even years later Rossi still had a much deeper understanding of the ensemble than anyone else in the profession.

The Admiralty moat was filled in around 1840 and the boulevard, which begins at Senate Square, was put in its place. In 1844 it was decided to place two bronze figures of the Winged Victory, which had been brought from Berlin, at the entrance of the boulevard. Accompanying the sculptures was a design for their supporting columns, prepared by a German artist named Rauch. The figures were small, shallow in detail, and not at all suitable for their intended location. Since at that time the western part of Senate Square could be seen from Admiralty Square and Dvortsovaia Square, the spatial significance of the bronze figures within the general system of the ensemble of the central squares was considerable.

The great master, who had designed and built a sizeable portion of the central ensemble of St. Petersburg but who had now fallen into disfavor, was "ordered on highest authority, to prepare a cost estimate on the basis of the enclosed sketch" drawn by an unknown and insignificant German artist, who had not even seen the site on which the columns bearing the sculptures were to be placed. With a clear understanding of the requirements of the ensemble and with remarkable dignity Rossi replied:

> During the examination of the drawings of the columns and statues prepared by Rauch, I discovered that they will be out of scale with the large space of the square where they are to be placed . . . for which reason their size should be adjusted. . . . [On] the other hand, if the height of the columns were to be increased they would appear to be out of scale with the statues. . . . [In] order to eliminate all these discrepancies, and in order to correct the disproportionality of the said columns I suggest that they be left without the

square bases, and that the bronze capitals and base steps be eliminated and a pedestal be created in their place. In connection with the above I take the liberty of proposing the following:

1. . . . It is incorrect to place them within the side alleys of the boulevard. I suggest that they be placed flanking it, and facing each other, on single pedestals without steps, and in proportion not only to the statues on top, but also to their surroundings.

2. I find it equally important that these statues . . . without the steps and placed on granite pedestals . . . be placed on the side and flanking the newly built bridge across the Neva, and I consider it a great privilege to submit drawings prepared by myself showing the boulevard and the columns together with the statues in two perspective views . . . indicating at the same time the manner in which I propose to place the statues on top of the columns and . . . the pedestals.[13]

Rossi's argument was certainly correct, but Rauch's drawings had already been approved and to the detriment of the architectural appearance of Admiralty Boulevard "His Majesty confirmed that the two bronze figures be placed on columns . . . according to the drawings sent from Berlin, and that the columns be located according to the sketches accompanying those drawings." Later the area of the central squares was divided into separate parts by the trees of the public park in front of the Admiralty, and the scale discrepancies together with the unsuitable location of the two monuments became less apparent. However, at that time their disproportions were obvious.

These were the most important projects in the reconstruction of Senate Square in terms of their architectural significance within the central ensemble of the city.

In connection with the reconstruction of St. Isaac Cathedral, Montferrand proposed that the monument of Peter I be relocated at the point of intersection of the axes of Senate and Admiralty squares. He made several proposals, the second of which placed the monument at the intersection of both the central axis of the cathedral and that of the Admiralty side-wing. Fortunately none of these proposals was realized, since even the best of them would have been to the detriment of the Bronze Horseman. The location of this monument had been carefully selected in the first place by its creator, Fal-conet.[14] Disregarding the fact that all the buildings around Senate Square had been rebuilt since the erection of the monument, the spatial relationships—such as its juxtaposition to the Neva and the quays—had remained the same. Fortu-nately, Montferrand's proposals were not realized, and the Bronze Horseman was the only element within the huge spaces of the central squares which did not conform to their strict geometrical layout as laid down by the masters of the 19th century. The unique and inimitable charm of Falconet's siting is based precisely on the noncompliance to the strict axiality of all the other elements within the space of the central squares, and thus underlines even more the spatial significance of the monument within the regular structure of the ensemble.

After its reconstruction Senate Square became an integral part of the system of the five central squares. Its architec-tural ties with the rest of the ensemble were provided first, by the elevation of the Riding Academy, which closed the view from both Admiralty and Dvortsovaia squares; and second, by the architectural character of the Senate and Synod façades which were designed in harmony with all of the surrounding buildings within the central area of the ensemble. Finally, the choice of the center line between the Senate and Synod fa-çades and the exterior limit of Admiralty Boulevard as the long axis rather than the center line between the Admiralty and Senate and Synod façades, gave the square the same geometrical set of coordinates as Admiralty Square and Razvodnaia Square.

The last, and also the least successful, effort was the reconstruction of St. Isaac Square. It was started in 1839 with the construction of the Mariinski Palace, and was concluded with the erection of a monument to Nikolai I, both coinciding with the completion of St. Isaac Cathedral.

The following directive, dated April, 1738, is recorded in one of the documents of the Commission for Regular Construction in St. Petersburg: "In the area between the Moika and Admiralty Field a gap is to be left between the buildings for a market square." [15] St. Isaac Square assumed its triangular shape as a result of this directive remaining unchanged for almost a hundred years. However, trade did not develop in the square and the Commission for the Stone Construction of St. Petersburg and Moscow proposed its subdivision for building development. This project was not realized. But in 1820 Montferrand built the house of Count Lobanov-Rostovski (later the building of the Military Ministry) on the triangular lot between St. Isaac Cathedral and Voznesenski Prospect.

Before reconstruction, the plan of St. Isaac Square was basically triangular and it was surrounded primarily by two-story structures. In 1819, when the project for the Mikhailovski Palace was proposed, it was first suggested that the palace be built on St. Isaac Square, on the same site on which the architect Stakenschneider finally built the Mariinski Palace in 1845. Rossi did the general planning of the square, but the location of the proposed Mikhailovski Palace was eventually changed.

After the Mariinski Palace had been completed it was found to be totally cut off from the square by the houses located on the other side of the Moika. It was therefore decided to open up the square toward the palace with the result

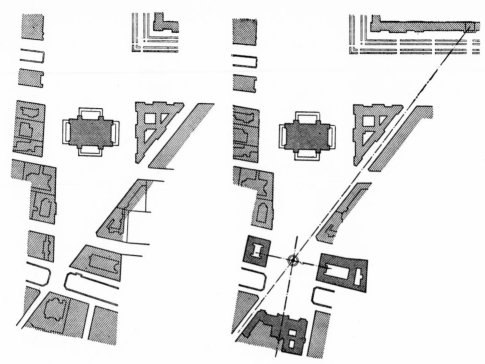

40. Plan of St. Isaac Square. Left: Before reconstruction. Right: After reconstruction.

that the part to be demolished had to be replanned. At that time the architect, N. Efimov, built two ministerial complexes near the Moika. These two projects completed Rossi's plan of 1819 without introducing any major changes (see illustration 40). Although Rossi was in disfavor and had no commissions at the time, it still became necessary to seek his authoritative advice during the reconstruction of the square. In 1841 the minister of the imperial court, Volkonski, issued a communiqué which announced that His Royal Highness "had chosen to appoint, henceforth, the architect K. Rossi as a member of all the construction commissions presently attached to H. M. Cabinet." [16]

As a result of this new construction the spatial unity of the square was destroyed; its outlines became jagged and irregular and it was in effect divided into two separate areas. The area near the cathedral was for a long time surrounded by low buildings and served as a circulation link between the cathedral and the new developments in the other parts of the square.

Rebuilt by Stakenschneider and Efimov under Rossi's supervision and according to his general plan, St. Isaac Square was the last comprehensive planning project to be carried out in the center of old St. Petersburg. Its reconstruction marks the beginning of the decline of the art of city building in Russia. Even though only two architects were commissioned, and even though they built at the same time and in the same place, no architectural unity was achieved between their projects. The location of the ministries within the ensemble of St. Isaac Square was predetermined by Rossi's general plan and may be considered their best feature.

Judged as individual works of architecture the new ministries are good solutions. Their façades are similar; the slight variation in architectural expression and detail creates additional architectural variety and interest; and their general appearance from the Moika is quite pleasant. However, their architectural relationship to the palace and the cathedral is extremely poor.

It must be admitted that before its reconstruction the space of the square was badly defined and that the buildings around it represented a diversity of architectural styles but fortunately these deficiencies were less apparent within the space of the square itself. The mass of the cathedral is so large and dominates the space of the square so clearly that any other elements beside it are reduced to secondary importance. Thus, in terms of architectural significance, the space of the square is secondary, whereas the mass of the cathedral is, without a doubt, its primary element.

In 1859, after completion of the reconstruction, a statue of Nikolai I was placed on the square. The sculptor was P. Klodt, and A. Montferrand designed the pedestal. Documents and sketches show that Montferrand planned to place the monument in front of the south portico of the cathedral. The location was approved by the court, but the Holy Synod protested, mainly because of the position of the horse. The objection was that the horse and the rider were placed in such a way that their combined rears were turned toward the entrance to the cathedral. It was suggested that the sculpture be placed closer to the portico with its front facing the cathedral and its rear turned toward the square. But this idea was dismissed as equally unsatisfactory. Finally the statue was placed on the axis of the cathedral and slightly left of the axis of Voznesenski Prospect so as not to obstruct the view toward Admiralty Tower.

This concludes the reconstruction—begun in the first half of the 19th century—in and around the five central squares which now became the central ensemble of St. Petersburg.

9

Analysis of the system of the five central squares as a whole

The foregoing examination of the reconstruction work carried out within the central area of the city dealt with each square separately. It showed that the process of reconstruction can be divided into two main periods. In the first phase the system of the "three prongs" was concluded with the reconstruction of the Admiralty. As mentioned earlier, it can be assumed that Zakharov was at that time not really concerned with achieving architectural unity between the Admiralty and the surrounding buildings. After the modification of Zakharov's general plan (the introduction of Admiralty Boulevard), the second phase of the reconstruction was initiated.

Its main aim was the unification of the central squares around the Admiralty into a spatial and architectural whole.

This chapter attempts to analyze the whole system and to answer the question as to whether a truly unified ensemble was indeed achieved. In general it appears that the planners of the reconstruction period strove to achieve such unity. Rossi's efforts, such as the General Staff Building and the buildings of the Senate and the Synod, give ample evidence of this. The individual features of these projects cannot be properly understood or explained without taking into account the whole system of the five central squares. Similarly, the creation of Admiralty Boulevard and the location of the Alexander Column can only be understood and explained within the context of the total ensemble. Many architects and, above all, the great master, K. Rossi, did much to achieve unity among the various separate elements of the central area.

Even after the completion of the reconstruction works, the Admiralty retained its position as the most important element of the central ensemble connecting the system of the five squares with the overall spatial structure of the city. Because of the large open spaces created around it, its dominance over the surrounding buildings was greatly diminished, while each separate square acquired its own spatial significance.

The main spatial characteristic of the five central squares is their mutual interpenetration and their gradual merging into one another. Each square enters the next: Dvortsovaia Square imperceptibly merges into Admiralty Square and Razvodnaia Square, Admiralty Square into Senate Square, and so on. The exact limits of the individual squares are difficult to determine, even though, in terms of their spatial groupings, they can be divided into three distinct architectural spheres of influence. The first group, consisting of Dvortsovaia Square, part of Dvortsovaia Quay, and Razvodnaia

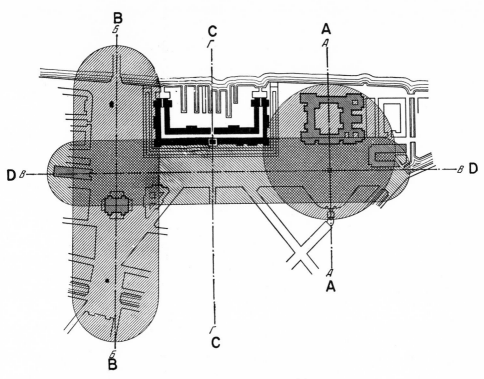

41. Plan of the five central squares and their axes of composition:
A-A, Dvortsovaia Square; B-B, Senate Square and St. Isaac Square;
C-C, Admiralty Square; D-D, main axis of the whole ensemble.

Square, gravitates toward the Winter Palace. The second group, consisting of Senate Square and St. Isaac Square, gravitates toward the large mass of the cathedral. Both of these groups are unified by the large space stretching between the Riding Academy and the Staff Building of the Imperial Guards, which represents the third spatial element of the ensemble. The composition of the general plan is based on the spatial equilibrium of these squares relative to the axis of symmetry of the Admiralty Building (see illustration 41).

This equilibrium is apparent not only in the general plan but also in the volumetric and spatial distribution of the gen-

eral building masses. The buildings around the squares—
with the exception of the three high elements—are neutral
in character and of almost equal height. The difference in
height between the Admiralty and the higher buildings surrounding it serves a specific purpose by providing the central
complex with an architectural frame. The spatial distribution
of the high dominants within the central area of the city helps
to emphasize the overall equilibrium of the system.

Thus, the first step toward the unification of the ensemble
was the creation of the central squares around its most important building, the Admiralty. This was effectively achieved
by their spatial interpenetration, the merging of one square
into the other, and the equilibrium of the various parts in
relation to the main architectural axis of the central complex.
The individual axes of the various squares are all related to
one another architecturally, thus binding the separate spaces
together into one unified complex. Each of them has been
analyzed separately in the previous chapters in the detailed
discussions of the various reconstruction works. Combined
into a single system, there is not one square which is not in
some way connected to the other. The location of the axes
of the three squares surrounding the Admiralty best illustrates
the soundness of this concept. The axes of Senate Square, Admiralty Square, and Razvodnaia Square are determined by
the center line between the outer edge of Admiralty Boulevard and the façades of the buildings opposite the Admiralty
on all three sides. The spatial significance of the Admiralty
is thus accentuated even more. The termination of the major
axes of the ensemble by monumental architectural elements
further strengthens the spatial integration of the squares.

The composition of each square is organized around a
major and a minor axis, with definite architectural relationships created between them. Without this, there would be no

composition. Within the ensemble of the five central squares the Admiralty is without doubt the most important element. This is due to its large size, its architectural monumentality, and the quality of its architectural detail, as well as to its key function within the spatial structure of the city. All these factors prove the validity of the general design concept. The Admiralty represents the central source from which all the other spaces emanate.

The two most important squares of the ensemble are Dvortsovaia Square and Senate Square, mainly because of their large size and the high quality of their architecture. Their relative importance within the structure of the ensemble should thus be analyzed first. Senate Square, which is open toward the Neva, is connected by a bridge to Vasilevski Island. The large bulk of St. Isaac Cathedral—which represents the architectural dominant of the city skyline—is part of its spatial structure. However, in terms of its monumental architecture, its individuality, and its spatial contrasts, Dvortsovaia Square must be considered even more interesting than Senate Square.

Admiralty Square has the character of a connecting element, and is, in fact, more of a "boulevard" between Dvortsovaia Square and Senate Square than a full-blown square. St. Isaac Square and Razvodnaia Square are less important, partly because of their smaller size, and partly because they are less successful architecturally.

The relative significance of all these squares within the central ensemble is thus a function of their individual spatial and architectural characteristics. Dvortsovaia Square is a good example. Even though both the Winter Palace and the opposite building of the General Staff are major architectural statements, superbly designed and well related in massing and detail, the large and serene open space between them is nevertheless the dominant spatial element of the square. The Alexander Column helps to emphasize the importance of the vast area of the open square even more. Thus, in every respect Dvortsovaia Square is unique among the other squares of St. Petersburg. The rest of the squares—such as the one in front of the Kazan Cathedral, in front of the Mikhailovski Palace, or in front of the Alexander Theater—are merely secondary spatial elements representing the architectural setting for a major building or a complex of buildings. In the case of Dvortsovaia Square the space literally "precedes" the palace.

The space of Senate Square tends to gravitate strongly toward the huge mass of the cathedral, however, since it is open toward the Neva at its opposite end; it also includes the large panorama of the Neva basin and beyond. Consequently one may speak about the definite subordination of such elements as form, size, the quality of the architectural solution, spatial hierarchy, etc., to an overall single concept. The approaches to the squares and the architectural treatment of the circulation links within the system are additional elements helping to determine the general structure of the ensemble.

There are six major approaches to the central ensemble, namely the three radials from the interior of the city, the two approaches from the Neva waterfront, and the entry via the arch from Nevski Prospect to Dvortsovaia Square. All of these approaches are functionally well situated, and their planning is excellent both as far as circulation and their spatial distribution are concerned. It should also be mentioned that they were conceived under extremely difficult circumstances owing to the complexity of existing conditions as well as the other restrictions described earlier.

A few examples will illustrate this point further. In Rossi's scheme for the entrance from Nevski Prospect to Dvortsovaia Square, two arches were to be constructed. One of these had to be designed as a double arch because of the odd angle formed by the street, making his task even more difficult. Zakharov took considerable structural risks when he added to the bulk of the Admiralty Tower to make it the focal point of the "three prongs." The differential settlement of the foundations shortly after Zakharov's death represented the structural aspect of Zakharov's gamble. The architectural risks were equally great. By making the tower a distinct and separate element of the general composition he suppressed "almost" all of its architectural links with the horizontal body of the main complex. But it was precisely this "almost" which made his work a masterpiece and not just another "good" piece of architecture.

The architectural development of the Neva waterfront has an equally interesting history and is closely related to the evolution of the ensemble of the central squares. Rossi worked under considerably more complex conditions than his predecessor, Zakharov. His brilliant plan for the Senate and Synod project is a striking example of his architectural skill and his ability to solve the many contradictions inherent in the problem.

The architectural organization of the major circulation paths within the system of the central squares was solved by making the axis of St. Isaac Cathedral coincide with the axis of the bridge across the Neva, by "adjusting" the orientation of the Riding Academy with respect to the perspective view from Dvortsovaia Square, and by the skillful placement of the Alexander Column at the opposite end. The faultless organization of the major circulation paths was a direct result of their functional response to actual conditions during reconstruction.

The next question to be asked is how Rossi and other architects of that period succeeded in achieving architectural unity among the various buildings of the ensemble.

The reconstruction projects carried out in the first half of the 19th century obviously did not include all the buildings within the area of the central ensemble. To talk about the architectural unity among all the buildings in this part of the city is therefore impossible. Moreover, even among the new projects a number of individual buildings do not fit the general pattern. The lack of architectural unity between St. Isaac Cathedral and its immediate surroundings is one example, the poor relationship between the Mariinski Palace and the ministries designed by Efimov is another.

In the main areas of reconstruction, however, the planners did achieve architectural unity and the spatial interrelationships within the ensemble are generally successful (see illustration 42). The buildings along Dvortsovaia Quay were conceived as a unified composition even before the reconstruction of the central squares was begun. After the reconstruction of Dvortsovaia Square the architectural coherence among the buildings of the eastern part of the central ensemble was further reinforced. In the western part of the ensemble the large mass of the cathedral completely dominates its surroundings and particularly the space of the two squares to the south and north. This makes the architectural diversity of the buildings around these squares less conspicuous. However, the further one moves away from the cathedral, the less its direct architectural influence is felt. In terms of overall unity within the general ensemble it was more important to achieve architectural harmony between the buildings located at the

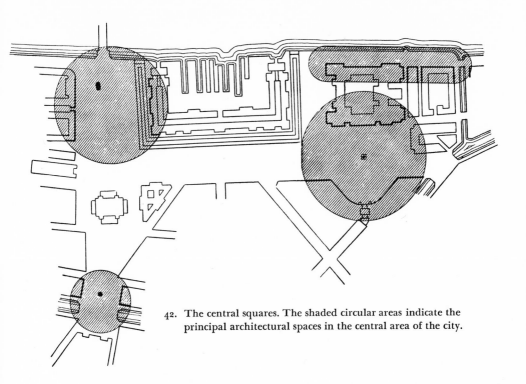

42. The central squares. The shaded circular areas indicate the
principal architectural spaces in the central area of the city.

opposite ends of the squares south and north of the cathedral
(i.e., Senate Square and St. Isaac Square), this being subsequently realized by the reconstruction works of Rossi and
Efimov.

Let us sum up the conditions which made the central ensemble of St. Petersburg unique and which were indispen-
sable to the creation of its spatial and architectural unity:

1. The creation of a system of squares around the Admiralty,
   and the spatial equilibrium of this system with respect to
   the main axis of the central area of St. Petersburg.
2. The spatial unification of the squares by means of an
   intricate system of axial relationships.
3. The subordination of secondary elements to the major
   spatial elements of the ensemble.

4. Spatial and structural hierarchy, and the articulation of significant elements within the various spaces of the central ensemble.
5. Architectural unity among the important spatial link elements.
6. Proper visual orientation and correct spatial distribution of the principal avenues of access and the main circulation paths of the ensemble.

Thus, in the middle of the 19th century, the system of the five central squares of St. Petersburg represented a unified architectural whole (see illustration 44).

In summing up, it may be said that the central ensemble was characterized not only by its formal and architectural unity but also by its important function in the political and social life of the city; by the quality of its architectural detail, as well as by its special position in the spatial structure of St. Petersburg. Its architectural character reflected the ideological and political convictions of its ruling classes. Equally important was its spatial relationship to the other ensembles in the central part of the city and its significance in the general silhouette of the capital.

The political significance of the ensemble of the five central squares was reflected by the type and function of the buildings surrounding them. These were: the Winter Palace, at that time the official residence of royalty; the building of the Army's General Staff; the building of the Staff of the Imperial Guards; the Senate, representing the highest lawmaking body; the Holy Synod, representing the State Church; St. Isaac Cathedral, the largest church in St. Petersburg; the Military Ministry; the Ministry of Foreign Affairs; the Finance Ministry; the ministries of Agriculture and State Properties; the building of the State Council (the Mariinski Palace); and the palace of the Governor of St. Petersburg. The political significance of these buildings is self-evident and it is quite obvious that the area of the central squares represented the political center of the capital and the nation.

The main function of the huge squares was the staging of parades designed to demonstrate the strength and might of Russia (see illustration 43). On ordinary days Admiralty Boulevard and Nevski Prospect were very popular strolling avenues for the fashionable set of St. Petersburg. On holidays the number of strollers doubled. If one also considers the driving, riding, boating, and skating along the Neva, the numerous exhibitions in the Riding Academy and the religious processions around St. Isaac Cathedral, one can see that the ensemble of the five central squares represented the center of political and social life for the city population in general and the ruling classes in particular.

The architectural expression of the central ensemble is the result of the combination of many diverse elements into a single whole, including its enormous dimensions, the severe character of its architecture, and the synthesis of its decorative elements.

A few dimensions will demontsrate the huge size of the central squares. The overall dimension from the Staff of the Imperial Guards to the Riding Academy is approximately 1,000 meters (3,280 ft.). The width of the space in front of the Admiralty is 152 meters (498.6 ft.), and the distance from the Winter Palace to the archway of the General Staff Building opposite is 230 meters (754.5 ft.). The distance from the portico of St. Isaac Cathedral to the edge of the Neva is 360 meters (1,181 ft.), and the size of Senate Square measured from the sidewing of the Admiralty to the arch between the Senate and Synod is 225 meters (738 ft.). The general area occupied by the five central squares is approximately 40 hectares (478,400 sq. yds.).[1] The five central squares are not

43. The ensemble of the central squares after reconstruction, showing one of the numerous military parades in progress.

only the largest ones in St. Petersburg, but also surpass in size those of Paris, Berlin, and Rome.

The architectural expression and the combination of plastic, ornamental, and decorative elements, helped to reveal more fully the spiritual significance and the artistic character of the ensemble. The architectural picture is completed by the inclusion of such works of art as the Bronze Horseman by Falconet, the Chariot of Victory by Demut-Malinovski and Pimenov, the Admiralty frieze (with a bas-relief depicting Neptune's allegorical award to Peter I of the power to rule the sea), and many others. To the extent to which these works participated in the solution of architectural problems they became an integral part of an organic whole.

The artistic merit of the individual works varies. Often their intention, as reflected in their subject matter, is the immortalization of the various monarchs. But in addition there are many artistic interpretations of such important events in Russian history as: the war with Sweden which made Russia a great European power, the victories over Napoleon, and other events celebrating the patriotism of the Russian people. In their integration with the architecture of the ensemble of the five central squares these works of art were superior to any others in St. Petersburg. They form an inseparable part of the whole picture.

Apart from some faults, the spatial and architectural unity of the central squares is beyond dispute. It was achieved by relatively simple and logical methods. The most important of these is the direct architectural termination of the long perspectives. This may be considered as the most characteristic feature of Russian classicism of the 19th century. The whole system of the central ensemble of the five squares is developed according to this concept and so are other parts of the plan of St. Petersburg. Almost all the buildings along the Neva waterfront and a number of other projects along Nevski Prospect are terminated by means of a direct closure at the end of a long perspective. The existence of many axes of symmetry defining individual spaces and ultimately subordinated to the main axis of the whole ensemble is another characteristic of 19th-century classicism. There are sixteen minor axes of symmetry in the ensemble of the five central squares and all of these are subordinated to the central axis of the Admiralty which at the same time represents the main axis of the central part of the city.

The masters of Russian classicism knew how to articulate the main structures of the ensemble by emphasizing their monumentality and architectural importance which, in turn, made the mediocrity of the rest of the surrounding buildings less apparent. In comparison with the classicism of the 18th century, the designs of Zakharov, Voronikhin, Thomon, and Rossi are more powerful, sometimes even brutal. De la Mothe, Feldten, and Quarenghi connected one building with the other in the manner of a "unified façade," so that the emergence of the total concept was realized only gradually. By contrast, the masters of the 19th century preferred to solve the problem by the introduction of a limited number of monumental buildings, located in strategic positions.

The art of the 18th century was the art of the jewel-like, narrow, but complete project. The art of the 19th century was characterized by concentration on important focal areas. If one compares the better sections of Dvortsovaia Quay with the Exchange by Thomas de Thomon on the Strelka of Vasilevski Island, one can readily perceive the differences between these two approaches.

The location and the function of the ensemble of the five central squares within the spatial structure of the city is unique. In the middle of the 19th century the general spatial structure of St. Petersburg was complex and unbalanced, an expression of the uneven development of the city during the one and a half centuries of its existence. The various sections of the city, such as the Admiralty District, the Vasilevski District, and the Petersburg District were more or less independent fragments of the general plan of the capital. The spatial structure of the center was determined by the Neva waterfront, the "three prongs," the quays of the Moika, the Ekaterinski Canal, and the Fontanka. In the system of the "three prongs" Nevski Prospect was the most important. It was, in fact, the main boulevard of St. Petersburg.

A thorough analysis would be incomplete without some consideration of the relationship among the system of the central squares, the system of the quays, and the system of the "three prongs." One must also consider the outline of architectural elements in the general skyline of St. Petersburg.

Most of the Neva waterfront was developed during the 18th century, with the sole exception of three important buildings which were added during the reconstruction period in the 19th century. These were the Exchange on the Strelka, the Gornyi Institute, and the ensemble of the central squares. The Exchange on the Strelka, together with the Gornyi Institute, completed the perspective along the Neva, while the ensemble of the five squares completed the composition of the central area, namely the Admiralty District (see illustration 44).

The ensemble along the Neva shorelines can be divided into two parts. The left shore is characterized by a unified front of buildings of extreme geometrical clarity and continuity and consists of Angliiskaia Quay, the five central squares, and Dvortsovaia Quay. In contrast to the left shore of the Neva, the right one presents a more lively panorama. Here, the shoreline itself is highly irregular, the perspectives

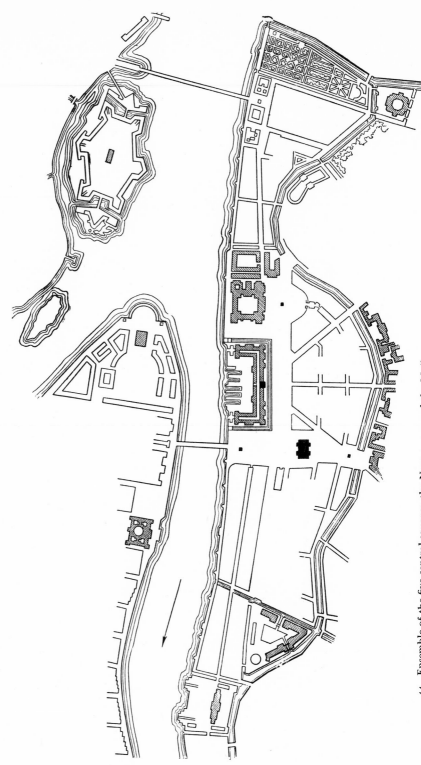

44. Ensemble of the five central squares, the Neva quays and the Moika.

are varied, and as one looks across the Neva basin the contrast between the opposite sides is made even more evident by the geometric-linear character of the quays of the central ensemble.

The spatial relationship between the central ensemble and the system of the quays along the left bank of the Neva is of great importance. Dvortsovaia Quay balances Angliiskaia Quay with respect to the central axis of the Admiralty, thus further emphasizing its spatial significance. The spaces which open toward the Neva, such as Senate Square, Razvodnaia Square, and the open court of the Admiralty were clearly articulated architecturally and provide a spatial contrast to the solid front of the "unified façade" along the waterfront. The primary role of the city center was rendered even more prominent by the use of the architectural concept of a "unified façade" along the Neva waterfront. The actual length of the façades of the buildings along Dvortsovaia and Angliiskaia quays is rather modest. This is one of the chief reasons why the huge, one kilometer (3,280 ft.) space of the five central squares produces such a strong visual impression and makes the central ensemble stand out among the other buildings on the left bank of the Neva—all the way from the Summer Garden to the Nikolaevski Bridge.

The view from the left bank provides two main areas of interest: the waters of the Bolshaia Neva from the Exchange on the cape of Vasilevski Island leading the eye toward the mouth of the river in the distance; and the large lakelike water expanse in front of the Winter Palace.

The most important buildings along the University Quay—the Academy of Arts and the Gornyi Institute—are clearly visible from both Senate and Razvodnaia squares. The mooring bollards and the activities associated with harbor life gave a lively character to this quay. The powerful portico by

Voronikhin completes the overall picture. Despite these features, however, it could never compete with the greater architectural significance of the ensemble of the five central squares.

The second part of the panorama is made up of the Exchange on the Strelka and the Peter and Paul Fortress on the Petersburg side. Both are large in size and monumental in character. Spatially they complement the Dvortsovaia waterfront, and are thus an integral part of the central ensemble. In terms of their location, and according to the original intentions of the masters of the 18th century, this ensemble was intended to become the center of St. Petersburg. However, this did not happen so that the two large complexes compete architecturally with the buildings of the central squares.

In terms of the distribution of its central spaces, 19th-century St. Petersburg could be compared to Venice in the 16th and 17th centuries. In both cities the most important buildings were part of a system of central squares, and in both cases these squares were located along the waterfront, facing another important architectural complex on the opposite shore. The colorful life of Venice was reflected in the water surface in front of the [San Marco] Piazzetta. In St. Petersburg the central squares opened toward the wide basin of the Neva in a similar fashion. Admiralty Court was filled with anchoring ships, their high masts and fluttering pennants rising into the sky. In both cases, capes project into the central bay. However, in Venice the cape development does not compete architecturally with the ensemble of the central squares as it does in St. Petersburg. The composition of the Strelka is architecturally self-contained and spatially self-sufficient. The architecture of the Strelka is not subordinated to the character of the other buildings along the right bank of the Neva, and the Exchange seems to "turn away" from the palace and the central squares, while at the same time competing with the buildings on the other side.

Thus the architectural character of the Neva waterfront within the central area of the city is based on the architectural contrast of the opposite shores. The left bank represents the well-ordered part of the city center. The right bank is characterized by its picturesque silhouette which can be seen from Razvodnaia Square, Senate Square, Dvortsovaia Quay, Angliiskaia Quay, and from the windows of the royal palace. The complexity of this solution is largely based on the subordination of the features of the site to the geometrically structured main part of the ensemble.

There is no doubt about the fact that the system of the central squares represented the dominant element within the whole mainland area of St. Petersburg. All the important buildings were concentrated within the area toward which they converged and in which they terminated. Other nodal elements such as the Marsovo Pole drill grounds, the Summer Garden, and the various squares adjoining Nevski Prospect were secondary spaces and complementary to the ensemble of the central squares. Without these secondary spaces the central ensemble would have appeared out of scale and unrelated to the regular building masses in the rest of the city. The secondary ensembles within the Admiralty District were in fact conceived as architectural transition elements between the regular construction of the side streets and smaller squares, and the main ensemble of the capital, and were subordinate to it both in scale and architectural significance. The high elements within the central area—the tower of the Admiralty and the dome of St. Isaac Cathedral—had considerable influence on the formation of the architectural image of these subsidiary ensembles. In this connection it is important to mention the architectural organization of the quays of the

Moika, the Ekaterinski Canal (now called the Griboedov Canal), and the Fontanka.

The Moika has its beginning at the Summer Garden and circles smoothly around the ensemble of the central squares. Its peculiar charm is based on the contrast between its curvature, the straight lines of the boulevards, and the ordered geometrical shapes of the squares. Many of the large and significant buildings of the city are located near the Moika, and their architectural image is to a large degree determined by this juxtaposition. Moreover, the Moika has existed as an independent architectural organism from the founding of St. Petersburg to the present. In this sense it "holds up a mirror" to the central area, the Marsovo Pole, the Summer Garden, and the New Holland area. From the Zimnaia Kanavka (the little Winter Canal) to the Novaia Gollandia (the New Holland) the Moika quays are architecturally unified and spatially subordinated to the ensemble of the central squares. This was achieved by reserving the section between Nevski and Voznesenski prospects along the Moika quays for important palaces and by recessing them behind the general line of buildings, thus providing these spaces with their special architectural character.

There is another important aspect which reinforces the spatial significance of this area: when one walks along this section of the Moika the tower of the Admiralty can be glimpsed three times, providing a direct visual connection with the central complex. The row of the palaces is terminated by St. Isaac Square which also opens toward the Moika. The large dome of the cathedral thus becomes an integral part of the architectural structure of the ensemble along the Moika, masking to a large degree the architectural disorder along other parts of its quays. Quite obviously the architectural potential of the Moika quays has not been fully exploited. Apart from the important complexes and the row of palaces near the central area many sections along its banks are architecturally insignificant and not related to each other. In these areas the granite retaining walls, the railings, the arched bridges, and the steps down to the water are the only architectural "link elements" which hold the whole composition together. Their best features are the stone retaining walls and the iron gratings. These provide a continuity with the whole which would otherwise be lacking. The arched stone bridges and the stairs down to the water represent another pleasant feature of the Moika quays. But it is the space of the five central squares which acts as the main unifying element, tying the fragments along the Moika together and reflecting the architectural influence of the central ensemble along its whole length.

The architectural development along the Fontanka and the Ekaterinski Canal in the middle of the 19th century is equally interesting, but unfortunately beyond the scope of this book. Suffice to say that, like the Moika, both the Fontanka and the Ekaterinski Canal sweep around the central ensemble in ever-wider arcs accentuating the formal geometry of its spatial structure. Each of them was developed simultaneously and each of them had its unique spatial structure. The most important architectural elements near Ekaterinski Canal are Kazan Cathedral, the Bank, Morski Cathedral and Nikolai Square. The spaces along the Fontanka are dominated by the dome of Troitski Cathedral. However, the spatial influence of the central squares is felt even here, despite the long distance from them. The spire of the Admiralty and the dome of St. Isaac Cathedral provide the visual links with the center and thus become part of the architectural image of the Fontanka and the Ekaterinski Canal. One could therefore say that it is as impossible to conceive of the architectural image of the canal without including the ensemble of the five central squares, as it is to imagine it without the many pedestrian bridges of which the Bankovski, the Tsepnyi, and Lvinyi are typical.

The system of the "three prongs" is terminated by the Admiralty Tower. The visual connection with the tower is the only architectural link between the central ensemble, Voznesenski Prospect, and Gorokhovaia Street. The main thoroughfare of St. Petersburg—Nevski Prospect—presents an entirely different case.

A complete inventory of all the various additions, alterations, and changes which took place along Nevski Prospect in the first half of the 19th century reveals the surprising fact that the boulevard was actually almost completely rebuilt during that period. The masters of 19th-century classicism, among these primarily Voronikhin and Rossi, made use of every new commission to transform the boulevard into a grand spatial composition consisting of an unbroken chain of related ensembles. With each new project the architects expanded the spatial connections between Nevski Prospect and the adjacent territories as well as the nearby complexes, thus transforming the boulevard into a complex spatial composition, subordinated both architecturally and spatially to the ensemble of the five central squares (see illustration 45).

The creation of the semicircular space in front of Kazan Cathedral by A. Voronikhin was the first in a chain of squares along Nevski Prospect. The large square is defined by a monumental semicircular colonnade which also helps to relate the adjacent streets to the spatial structure of the cathedral complex. Rossi was drawn into the planning of Nevski Prospect in 1818. To connect the newly constructed Troitski Bridge with Nevski Prospect, the large territories of the Imperial Gardens had to be cut up by the introduction of a

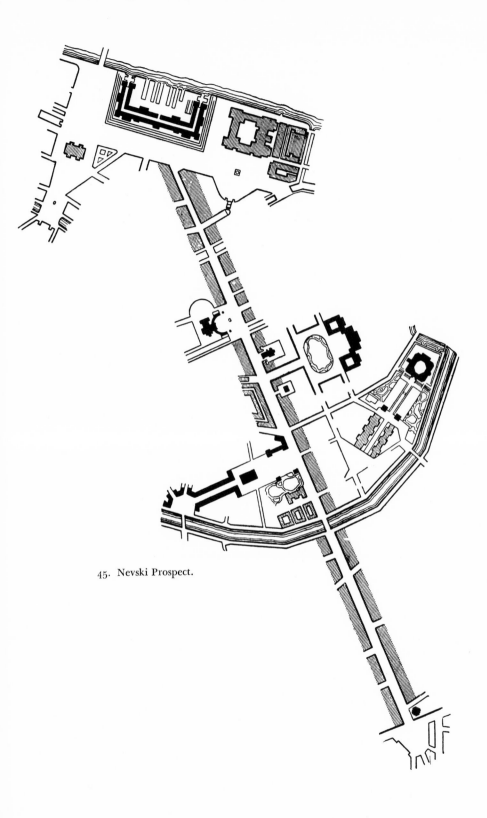

45. Nevski Prospect.

new traffic artery, and Sadovaia Street had to be extended as far as the Marsovo Pole. The street was planned by Rossi in such a way that the outline and the spire of Inzhenerni Castle could be seen from Nevski Prospect. This introduced the third tower element into the spatial organization of Nevski Prospect. During the same period Rossi also worked on the design of Mikhailovski Palace and its integration with the spatial structure of Nevski Prospect. The third major spatial element along Nevski Prospect—the Alexander Theater—was also designed by Rossi. He made more than ten proposals for the planning of the square in front of the theater. The main theme emerged only gradually, and he arrived at the final solution only after trying a number of architectural and spatial variations and combinations. The final scheme consisted of two squares connected by a street.

As a result of these activities Nevski Prospect was gradually developed into a unified architectural composition subordinated as a whole to the system of the central squares. This relationship was mainly the result of the spatial hierarchy realized by the chain of ensembles along Nevski Prospect which found their perceptual and architectural culmination in the large unified space of the five central squares. Without this gradual spatial build-up the huge size of the central squares would have appeared out of scale and overpowering with respect to the other spaces in the city. The function of Nevski Prospect as an architectural sequence building up to a climax in the space of the five central squares was superbly accomplished by the manipulation of the architectural character and the spatial hierarchy of the various projects flanking the boulevard, becoming ever more powerful and intense toward the center of the city.

Within the limits defined by the present Ploshchad Vostania and the Admiralty Tower, Nevski Prospect can be divided into three distinct parts. These are defined by the Fontanka and the Moika, which in turn are accentuated by the elegantly arched bridges. The first portion, extending from the Ploshchad Vostania to the Fontanka, was at that time still unfinished. It was started at the beginning of the 19th century and has the character of an ordinary street flanked by two rows of continuous façades without accents or interruption. Beyond Anichkov Bridge the boulevard abruptly changes its character. In contrast to the severity of the preceding section with its corridor-like feeling, and apart from the geometrical layout of the overall plan, we have here an environment which is essentially picturesque both in plan and in the character of its architectural appearance. Various squares open to the left and the right, and, recessed from the street, we can see the large masses of the heterodox churches. It is from here that one may catch another glimpse of the Admiralty Tower in the distance: the dark opening of the entrance arch, the silhouette of the tower, and, crowning all, the golden needle of the spire.

The third and last portion of the boulevard again differs dramatically from the preceding one. At first it narrows, and the character of the buildings facing the boulevard becomes more modest and restrained. The perspective is clearly directed toward the tower and nothing intervenes to deflect the eye. At the end of the boulevard the buildings become higher, making the street appear even narrower. Through the gap one can see the tower and a small part of the wings of the Admiralty. The space of the square cannot be perceived until the last moment when one has left the boulevard behind.

This gradual unfolding of all the compositional elements of Nevski Prospect would remain incomprehensible without its grand culmination in the vast spaces of the ensemble of central squares. Both the complex of the central squares and that of Nevski Prospect have one thing in common: their architectural and spatial sphere of influence extend far beyond their actual dimensional limits. Many adjacent streets and a great number of the surrounding building masses thus become an organic part of these two large spatial systems.

A definite spatial hierarchy exists in the sense that the open space of the Neva is as much an integral part of the ensemble of the central squares as the many large and small squares in front of the various churches in the central part of the city: the views along the Fontanka, the Ekaterinski Canal, and the Moika are equally an integral part of the spatial structure of Nevski Prospect. All this creates the impression of great spaciousness, which is in fact the main characteristic of St. Petersburg—a city of long, significant perspectives. The architectural and spatial importance of the ensemble of the central squares is also clearly expressed in the general skyline of the city.

In terms of absolute size, the highest buildings of the ensemble of the five central squares yield only to the overall height of the spire of the Peter and Paul Cathedral. However, it is quite obvious that in spite of its greater height this spire does not possess the same spatial importance as the dome of St. Isaac Cathedral or even the spire of the Admiralty Tower.

The skyline of St. Petersburg has two visual aspects, namely its appearance from within the city and from outside it. From within, the view of the spires is generally lost. From the Gulf of Finland and from the surrounding islands the dome of St. Isaac Cathedral is without question the dominating element of the city: it is rightly called the "golden cap" of St. Petersburg.

Perceived from the interior of the city, the spire of Peter

and Paul Cathedral relates well to the spire of the Admiralty. Their main difference is that the spire of the cathedral has only local importance. It does not act as the focal point of any distant perspective as does the Admiralty spire; its spatial influence is confined to its immediate surroundings and does not extend past the limits of the Neva water basin. The great height of the spire of Peter and Paul Cathedral is partially masked by the mass of buildings around the cathedral. The Admiralty Tower, which is the terminating element of the "three prongs," is spatially in a much more strategic location. Its spire can be seen from the very ends of each of the three radials. From the Neva the tower of the Admiralty rises together with the dome of St. Isaac Cathedral. It can be said without exaggeration that both the dome of St. Isaac Cathedral and the tower of the Admiralty establish the dominance of the ensemble of the five central squares in the overall silhouette of the city.

To sum up, the ensemble of the central squares represented the political and administrative center of St. Petersburg and the hub of the social and political life of the ruling classes. Its architectural form was the result of a synthesis with other elements of the fine arts, reflecting in a clear and powerful manner the significant events of Russian history in the 18th and the first half of the 19th centuries. The central ensemble represented the most important element within the spatial structure of the city and determined the planning of the whole Admiraly District. It is located at the point of convergence of the radials and simultaneously accomplishes their architectural termination. Finally, its high structures provide the dominant elements in the skyline of the city.

By virtue of all this the ensemble of the five central squares represented in the first half of the 19th century a fully developed architectural center for the city of St. Petersburg.

A number of architectural historians maintain that the Exchange on the Strelka of Vasilevski Island always has been and forever will be the architectural center of St. Petersburg. However, this view cannot be supported. It is incorrect, first, because the existing central part of the city at the present differs considerably from what it was during the first half of the 19th century. Great damage was done to the ensemble of the central squares during the latter half of the last century when the wharf inside the Admiralty was filled in and built up from the side of the Neva, and the continuity of the central space of the five squares was destroyed by the planting of trees in front of the Admiralty.

Secondly, this view is incorrect because it ignores the city as a living organism, constantly changing, growing and developing in different directions. True, during Peter I's time the architectural center was located around the central basin of the Neva, and its main element was indeed the Strelka of Vasilevski Island. It was still the architectural center during the second half of the 18th century, but its main element had even then moved to Dvortsovaia Quay. During the 19th century the architectural center of the city shifted completely to the other side of the Neva, and was defined by the system of the five central squares. It remained so until its disruption during the late 19th century, when the unity of the five central squares was destroyed by the addition of the park in front of the Admiralty.

Thirdly, this view is wrong because it ignores the economic, political, and cultural factors influencing the development of the city. According to this theory the Exchange would have had to remain the architectural center of Leningrad forever and all future projects would have had to be subordinated to this "eternal" center of the city.

Any valid analysis of the planning of St. Petersburg should

acknowledge the existence of the "other" parts of the city surrounding the central ensemble. Behind the splendid façades of the central part and in many other parts of the city there was overcrowding, lack of space, and incredible poverty. Block after block of tenements filled Sennaia Square near the Narva Gate, the Vyborg District, the Petersburg District, and many others.

During the reconstruction of St. Isaac Cathedral, the first political crisis already darkened the horizon of Russia's future. It also marked the beginning of the decline in the planning of St. Petersburg. (But such is not the subject of this essay.) It marked the end of an era and also the end of a brilliant chapter in the history of urban design and city planning.

Explanatory and reference notes

Please Note: The citation *TsGIAL* used below stands for Central State Historical Archives of Leningrad. Items followed by an asterisk are available in Russian only.

Translator's note

1. B. H. Summer, *Peter the Great* (New York: Collier Books, 1965), pp. 9–10.
2. M. P. Vyatkin, ed., *Sketches of the History of Leningrad* (Leningrad: The Academy of Sciences, 1955), Vol. I., pp. 40–42.*
3. V. Klyuchevski, *Peter the Great,* translated from Russian by Liliana Archibald (New York: Vintage Russian Library, 1961), p. 155.
4. D. M. Sturley, *A Short History of Russia* (New York: Harper & Row, 1964), p. 29.
5. Summer, *op. cit.,* p. 36.
6. A. Senkevitch, *St. Petersburg.* Paper presented to the Department of Architecture, Texas Technological College, Lubbock, Texas, 1966.
7. *Ibid.,* p. 11.
8. A. V. Bunin, "The General Plan and the Architectural Ensemble of Old Petersburg," *Russian Architecture,* ed. by V. A. Shkvarikov (Moscow: Academy of Sciences, 1940), p. 59.*
9. George H. Hamilton, *The Art and Architecture of Russia* (Maryland: Penguin Books, 1954), p. 59.
10. Senkevitch, *op. cit.,* p. 21.
11. S. P. Luppov, *The History of the Building of St. Petersburg in the First Quarter of the 18th Century* (Moscow: Academy of Sciences, 1957), pp. 23–24.*

12. Vyatkin, *op. cit.*, p. 169.
13. Senkevitch, *op. cit.*, p. 21.
14. Peter Steveni, *Petrograd, Past and Present* (London: Grant Richards Ltd., 1915).
15. *Ibid.*
16. Luppov, *op. cit.*, p. 25.
17. *Ibid.*, p. 27.
18. Senkevitch, *op. cit.*, p. 15.
19. Vyatkin, *op. cit.*, pp. 38–39.
20. Senkevitch, *op. cit.*, p. 21.
21. Luppov, *op. cit.*, p. 175.
22. *Ibid.*, pp. 176–77.
23. *Ibid.*, p. 176.
24. Bunin, *op. cit.*, pp. 60–61.
25. Luppov, *op. cit.*, pp. 177–78.

Chapter 1

1. I. Zholtovskii, "The Ensemble in Architecture," *Construction Gazette*, May 30, 1940.*
2. Peter I originally named the city Sankt Pieter Burkh (Dutch). Later it became known as St. Petersburg (the name used in this text). During World War I this was Russianized to Petrograd. Finally, after the Russian Revolution the city received its present name, Leningrad. Located 59°57′N and 30°19′E of Greenwich, it is the northernmost city of comparable size, occupying approximately 64,000 acres. Prior to World War II its length from east to west was approximately 15 miles and its width from north to south about 11.5 miles. At its highest point in the Vyborg District it is 15 to 30 feet above sea level, at its lowest near the delta 4 to 6 feet only. (From *The Large Soviet Encyclopedia*, XXXVI.) *
3. The total length of the Neva between Lake Ladoga and the Gulf of Finland is 41 miles. At some places—for instance, opposite the Smolny Monastery—it measures 2,100 feet across. Its largest branch is deep enough to admit sea-going vessels. The Neva has many smaller branches in the delta region including the Large Neva (Bolshaia Neva), the Small Neva (Malaia Neva), the Large Nevka (Bolshaia Nevka), the Small Nevka (Malaia Nevka), as well as a number of smaller streams later converted into canals such as the Fontanka, which owed its name to the fact that it supplied many of the fountains in the Summer Garden. Further along are the Catherine Canal (Ekaterinski Kanal), the Encircling Canal (Obvodnyi Kanal), and thirteen others.
4. Vasilevski Island was named for St. Basil.

5. *Strelka* means, literally, "little arrow-head or bolt," and refers throughout to the cape of Vasilevski Island.

6. P. N. Stolpianskii, *Peterburg* (St. Petersburg, 1918), pp. 8–9.*

7. Admiralty Island was originally called Teutsche Sloboda, literally, German Suburb, because its first settlers were German workers imported for their skills.

8. The Kunstkammer was designed by Matarnovi, Kiaveri, and Zemtsov, and housed the Academy of Sciences. Peter started the first national science museum on its premises as well as the first public library. The upper part was designed to serve as an observatory.

9. *Gostinyi Dvor* means literally "arcade"; actually, "bazaar" conveys its meaning more accurately.

10. Jean Baptiste Alexander Leblond. Born in Paris in 1679, he died in St. Petersburg in 1719. Leblond was a pupil of LeNotre. In addition to his plan for St. Petersburg he also drew plans for the Summer Garden and designed the Strelna Chateau. He decorated the Peterhof, surrounding it with gardens modeled on Versailles. Most of his designs have been preserved in the form of drawings only.

11. I. I. Golikov, *Supplements to the History of Peter the Great* (Moscow, 1790–97), XI, p. 245.*

12. P. Petrov, "Chief Architect Leblond," *The Journal of the Ministry of Roads and Communications,* 1896.*

13. Apparently Leblond exaggerated the danger of military attack on St. Petersburg. While he was working on the plans the Swedes had already suffered two major defeats: on land at Poltava in 1709; at sea at Hängöudd in 1714. The Russian fleet and the fortress of Kronstadt on the island of Kotlin were additional deterrents and would have made penetration of the delta from the direction of the sea almost impossible. This may well be another reason why Leblond's plan was not realized.

14. Leblond's fortifications would have been as high as the Kirov Stadium which now stands on Krestovski Island. Looking at the latter one can imagine how impressive Leblond's fortifications would have been, especially when enhanced by the projecting spires of the many churches within the city and the masts of the ships anchored in the harbor.

15. J. Leblond, *Explanatory Notes on the Project,* Library of the Academy of Sciences of the USSR, Leningrad.*

16. The work did not proceed with sufficient speed to suit the Tsar. He therefore ordered merchants, tradesmen, landowners, and masons to come forward and threatened heavy penalties for any who disobeyed. He wrote to Prince Romanovski asking him to send 2,000 thieves and to collect all prisoners who had been deported to Vologda and Siberia. Thus he obtained a veritable horde of workers. [P. Steveni, *Petrograd, Past and Present* (London: Grant Richards, 1915).]

17. J. Leblond, *op. cit.*

18. Domenico Trezzini, born in Astano in 1679, was of Swiss-French origin. He died in St. Petersburg in 1734. He spent some years at the Danish

Court and in Germany before becoming chief architect first to Peter I and then to Catherine I. Trezzini designed and built the basilica of St. Peter and St. Paul on Petersburg Island and the palace of Peter I in the Summer Garden. He built the Twelve Imperial Colleges and in 1715 presented Peter with the plans for the grandiose St. Alexander Monastery later built by his son Giuseppe Trezzini. [P. Miliukov, *Outlines of Russian Culture* (Philadelphia: University of Pennsylvania Press, 1943), III, pp. 17–18.]

19. A. Münther, *Idealstädte, Ihre Geschichte, v. 15–17 Jahrhundert* (Berlin, 1957).

Chapter 2

1. *Glukhoi,* solitary, lonely, dead end; *protok,* canal, water course.

2. *Sloboda* means suburb.

3. The commission was set up by a nominal ukase issued in the name of Anna I, Johanovna, replacing the old Commission of Building. Apart from the above-mentioned architects, its other members were: its director, Naryshkin; Count Golovkin; Izmailov; Major Rauch; Engineer of Hydraulics Minikh; and a number of others. The documents concerning its foundation and subsequent activities can be found in the St. Petersburg Senate Archives, *Book of Imperial Ukases,* XXXII, 30–45.*

4. Michael Zemtsov was the first Russian architect to gain renown. As a boy he was brought from Moscow and taught Italian so that he could serve as an interpreter to foreign artists. He studied architecture under Trezzini and worked as an assistant architect with Leblond's successor Michetti. After the latter left Russia in 1728 the young Russian was promoted to the rank of chief architect. He designed the church of St. Simeon and St. Anna on Mokhovaia Street—an imitation of Trezzini's cathedral of SS. Peter and Paul—and the graceful memorial building to house the yawl of Peter I. He died in 1743, and was replaced by Rastrelli in the work of palace construction.

5. Nevski Prospect is Leningrad's main thoroughfare, stretching nearly three miles, from the Admiralty to the Alexander Nevski Monastery, to which the street owes its name. In 1788 a decision was made to "name the Great Perspective Road, which runs from the Admiralty to the Nevski Monastery, the Nevski Perspective." Later the street came to be called the "Nevski Prospect." [P. Kann, *Leningrad* (Moscow: Foreign Languages Publishing House, 1959), p. 94.]

6. Novgorod Road is so named because long before the Great Northern War the territory of present-day Leningrad was part of the Novgorod lands. The part of Great Novgorod Road that is now Litovski Prospect linked the Russian villages which were scattered along the banks of the Neva with the other lands belonging to Novgorod. Near the present-day Taurida Gardens it split into several paths, which ran down to the Neva.

When the foundations of the city had been laid and work begun at the Admiralty Yard, the Great Novgorod Road, which had in the meantime fallen into decay, became crowded with carts carrying iron, canvas, ropes, oak, in short, everything that the shipyard needed for its operation. In order to reach the Admiralty, however, the carts had to go by a round-about way, along narrow paths unsuited for such a heavy flow of traffic. It was therefore decided to make a road linking the Admiralty Yard directly with the Great Novgorod Road, and in 1709 a path was cut through the sparse woods, later widened, paved after a fashion, and lined with ditches on either side. This became Nevski Prospect. *Viz.* an ukase by Peter I "concerning the new road to the monastery," dated October 2, 1718, and relating to the collection of tolls for the passage along Nevski Prospect. (*Ibid.*)

7. *Gorokhovaia Ulitsa*, the so-called street of nuts, a popular corruption of the name of Count Harrach, which in Russian is pronounced *gorokh*.

8. *Viz.* Plans of St. Petersburg, compiled by Khomanov and Otesov, 1718, and also the plan presented to the King of Sweden, dated 1722. The first two plans show the two outer radials, namely Voznesenski Prospect and Nevski Prospect, while in the latter plan the central radial makes its appearance for the first time.

9. Tsilov, *Historical Plans of St. Petersburg*, 1853.*

Chapter 3

1. *Concerning Stone Construction*, Collection in *TsGIAL*, Vol. VI.*

2. *Ibid.*, for the year 1774.

3. Members of the working staff from 1764–74—called architectural helpers—were: Gavrila Belianinov; Ivan Mikhailov; Aleksei Niels. In 1795 they were: Peter Demidov; Grigorii Dmitriev; Larion Shalin; Victor Firsov; Mikhail Leim (the son); and Aleksei Dobriakov.

4. The absence of stone buildings around the Kronberg on the Petersburg side is explained by the prohibition against building such structures in its vicinity, aimed at making the defense of the Peter and Paul Fortress easier from the dry land. This prohibition was lifted in 1809, when Finland was incorporated into the Russian Empire, and the border between Russia and Sweden moved to the Torneo River.

Chapter 4

1. George Feldten (also Veldten), German architect (1730–1801), credited with the design of the Old Hermitage, the Neva granite quays, and the ornamental ironwork of the fence of the Summer Garden. [P. Miliukov, *op. cit.*, pp. 20–21.]

2. I. Grabar, *History of Russian Art,* I (1911), 312–13.*

3. *Complete Collection of the Laws of the Russian Empire* (St. Petersburg, 1839), ukase dated February 8, 1765, dealing with the "building of houses in St. Petersburg between the Neva and the Moika according to the plan, and the various arrangements concerning this matter." *

4. J. B. Vallin de la Mothe (also Delamothe), chief architect of Empress Catherine I and Tsar Paul I. Born 1729, died 1800. In St. Petersburg he built the Catholic church of St. Catherine (1763), the storage house of New Holland (1765), the Academy of Arts (1757–65), the house of the Duke of Olenburg, and the two small palaces of the Hermitage adjoining the Winter Palace. De la Mothe also introduced the style of Gabriel into Russia. He was nominated professor of the Academy of Arts in St. Petersburg in 1767. [P. Miliukov, *op. cit.,* p. 20.]

5. I. Grabar, *op. cit.,* 315–16.

6. *Ibid.*

7. Giacomo or Jacopo Quarenghi. Born in 1744 in Valle Imagna, died in St. Petersburg in 1817. He was an emulator of Palladio, and came to Russia through the offices of Grimm. Later he became court architect to Catherine II, Paul I, and Alexander I. He built a number of large projects in St. Petersburg, Moscow, and the provinces. He also worked in Vienna and Munich. In St. Petersburg his most important works were: the large Gallery of Raphael (1780), the Hermitage Theater (inspired by the Olympic Theater of Palladio in Vicenza) built in the years 1783–87, the Imperial Bank (1783–88), the Exchange Palace (started in 1790), the Catholic church of the Maltese Order of St. Jerusalem (1798–1800), the Institute for Young Women of the Nobility (1806–09), the Riding Academy, the hospital, and the Arch of Alexander. He also completed the building of the Smolny Monastery which had been left unfinished by its designer Rastrelli. In Peterhof he built the English Palace (1781–91). He decorated the sidewing of the Imperial Court at Tsarskoe Selo and the Grand Palace of Alexander, also at Tsarskoe Selo, which is considered to be his masterpiece (1792–96). [P. Miliukov, *op. cit.,* pp. 22–23.]

8. Thomas de Thomon. Born in Paris, 1756, died in St. Petersburg in 1814. He was appointed court architect of the Emperor and built the Great Theater (1803) after the old one had been destroyed by fire in Catherine II's time. He also built the Maritime Exchange and the mausoleum of Peter I on the outskirts of the city (1810).

9. The planning projects mentioned in the text are preserved in the form of copies only. These were made in the 1840's and form part of a large collection known as the *Archive Meier,* see chapter 5, *n.* 2.

10. A. Bunin, and M. Kruglova, "Concerning the Architecture of a Capital City," *Academy of Architecture,* no. 1 (1936).*

11. F. Engel's, *Anti-Diuring, Gospolitizdat* (Moscow 1953), p. 22.

12. 1 arshin equals 28 inches.

13. "Collection of the Commerce-Collegia," *TsGIAL,* 2, CXCI, 92.*

14. *Ibid.,* p. 96.

15. *Ibid.*, p. 104.

16. Antonio Rinaldi. Born and died in Rome (1709–1794). In 1752 he was called to Russia by Elisabeth's favorite, Prince Razumovski. In St. Petersburg he built the famous Marble Palace (1768–85) which was offered by Catherine II as a gift to Gregory Orlov, and was also the first marble edifice in Russia. In 1765 he did the project and the model for the old St. Isaac Cathedral, which burned down in 1710. [P. Miliukov, *op. cit.*, p. 20.]

17. A great number of documents have been preserved dealing with the selection of the location of the monument, its design, its casting, and its final placement on the square. Initially it was proposed to place the monument in front of the Admiralty Tower, facing Gorokhovaia Street, but after long deliberations priority was given to Senate Square. A letter from Catherine II to Falconet (who, together with Maria Collot and Gordeev created the monument), dated August 31, 1773, is of great interest in this connection. In it she asked the sculptor to suggest the location of the monument. The unveiling of the monument was reported in the February 19, 1782, issue of the *St. Petersburg Gazette*.

18. *Complete Collection of the Laws of the Russian Empire* (St. Petersburg, 1839), ukase dated May 28, 1783.*

Chapter 5

1. *TsGIAL*, folio 1310, 1/1417, I(1763), p. 18.*

2. *Archive Meier, GMIRL*, Atlas III, Vol. 2, Chap. IV.*

3. Adrian Zakharov (1761–1811). Studied in Paris under Jean-Francois Thereze Chalgrin. In St. Petersburg he rebuilt the Admiralty (1806–23) and finished the Imperial Library, started by L. Rusca in 1810.

4. I. Grabar, *op. cit.*, III, 449.*

5. *Ibid.*, p. 450.

6. *Complete Collection of the Laws of the Russian Empire* (St. Petersburg, 1839), ukase dated May 3, 1816.*

7. "Collection of the Commerce-Collegia," *TsGIAL*, 341/501, M, p. 241.*

8. N. Vrangel, *The Russian Museum of Tsar Alexander III* (St. Petersburg, 1904), I–II, Preface.*

9. P. Stolpianskii, "Admiralty Island—the Workers' Park," *Old Petersburg* (St. Petersburg, 1923).*

10. *Ibid.*

11. Obviously the model would be of great interest to all students of the history of Leningrad. In the 1930's the Committee of Arts of the USSR asked the British National Museum about the possible whereabouts of the model. The museum replied that the model was no longer part of its collections. Presumably it had passed into private hands.

12. *Archive Meier, GMIRL*, Atlas VII, description.*

Chapter 6

1. N. Lansere, "A. Zakharov and his Admiralty," *Old Cities*, 1921, no. 12.*

2. *Military and Naval Archives of Leningrad, Collection of the Naval Ministry*, folio 3046.*

3. *Ibid.*

4. *Ibid.*, folio 3050, sheet 4.

5. V. Kurbatov, *Peterburg* (St. Petersburg, 1913), p. 318.*

6. *Military and Naval Archives of Leningrad, Collection of the Naval Ministry*, folio 3050, sheets 219–20.*

7. *Ibid.*, sheet 69.

8. P. Bodrovskii, *The History of the Lancer Regiment of the Royal Body Guards* (St. Petersburg, 1903), p. 330.*

9. "Tshiganov—to the Admiralty Department, 1808," *Military and Naval Archives of Leningrad, Collection of the Naval Ministry*, folio 3050, sheet 97.*

10. A communication of the superintendent of the court-commissariat office, Count Latto, to the Ministry of Naval Forces.*

Chapter 7

1. Carlo di Giovanni Rossi, designated Karl or K. Rossi in the text. Born December 18, 1775, in Naples and died April 6, 1849, in St. Petersburg. He was the son of an Italian danseuse, and passed most his life in Russia, where he first worked under the direction of V. Brenna. In 1816, after a stay in Moscow, he went to stay permanently in St. Petersburg. [P. Miliukov, *op. cit.*, pp. 24–25.]

2. Bartolomeo Francesco di Rastrelli. Born in Paris, approximately 1700, died in St. Petersburg, 1771. He studied in France, but took many of his ideas from southern Germany where the rococo style was rich in decorative elements. At the age of fifteen he went to St. Petersburg with his father, the celebrated Italian sculptor, Bartolomeo Carlo Rastrelli. The son became the favorite architect of Empress Elisabeth and the chief builder during her reign. In St. Petersburg he built the Summer Palace (1741–44), the Vorontsov Palace (1743–45), and the Razumovski Palace (1774), also the Smolny Monastery (started 1748 and finished after his death by Quarenghi in 1835). His masterpieces were the Cathedral of the Resurrection of Christ, and the Winter Palace (consisting of 1,500 rooms and the first truly monumental edifice of the Russian Empire), together with the extension of the Hermitage (1754–62). In the environs of the capital he built the residence of Anichkov, the palace of Prince Stroganov (1750–54), and also built or rebuilt the immense and elaborate imperial complex of the Peterhof Palace (1774–52) and Tsarskoe Selo (1749–56).

From 1744 to 1767 he built St. Andrew Cathedral in Kiev. [P. Miliukov, *op. cit.*, pp. 18–19.]

3. Catherine II brought her court back to St. Petersburg, summoning to her side many of the brilliant men of the continent. The old-fashioned Muscovites and some of the pleasure-loving nobles, vegetating on their estates in the lonely provinces, began to recognize the city's attractions. It was no longer necessary to compel the nobility to reside in the place where a second Zenobia reigned. Many flocked to the capital of their own will, and soon it became one of the gayest and most popular cities in Russia. At this time the population numbered approximately 300,000. Catherine carried out Peter's ideas on a scale that even he might have shrunk from. Under her rule, St. Petersburg attained symmetry and beauty. [P. Steveni, *op. cit.*, p. 42.]

4. The conditions of the competition were published in the February issue of the *St. Petersburg Gazette*, 1779, p. 168.

5. Ivan Starov (1743–1808). He studied at the Academy of Arts in St. Petersburg, and also in Paris under the guidance of Charles de Wailly. He designed the Taurida Palace (1770).

6. N. Bylinkin, "Old and New Ensembles in Leningrad" *Architecture of the USSR*, no. 2 (1939).*

7. The Alexander Column was designed by A. Montferrand and erected in 1834 in memory of the Russian victory in the war of 1812. The bronze figure of the angel of victory on top of the column is the work of B. Orlovski, and the reliefs are the work of I. Leppe and P. Svintsov.

Chapter 8

1. The Frenchman August Ricard (Count Montferrand), created a count by Alexander II, was born in Chaillot near Paris, 1786. He was the pupil of Percier and Fontaine. After receiving letters of recommendation from Prince Wolkenski in 1816, he left for St. Petersburg. He worked on the restoration of St. Isaac Cathedral from 1829 to 1839. He also designed the Alexander Column and did some repair work on the Winter Palace. He was named professor at the Academy of Arts in St. Petersburg. [P. Miliukov, *op. cit.*, p. 25.]

2. A. Montferrand, *St. Isaac Cathedral* (St. Petersburg, 1845).*

3. *Église de St. Isaac restaurée et augmentée d'après les ordres de l'Empereur et Roi par Auguste de Montferrand, Architecte de sa Majestée Imperiale, Chevalier de l'ordre Royal de la Légion d'honneur* (St. Petersburg, 1820).

4. "The Academy of Arts," *TsGIAL*, folio 130, p. 303.*

5. "The Academy of Arts, Notes of Architect Modiui," *TsGIAL*, folio 130.*

6. *Ibid.*, p. 23.

7. *Ibid.*, p. 36.

8. "The Academy of Arts, Report of the Committee to Alexander I," *TsGIAL*, folio 130, p. 101.*

9. *Complete Collection of the Laws of the Russian Empire*, ukase dated February 11, 1824.*

10. "The Academy of Arts," *TsGIAL*, folio 130, p. 310.*

11. "Cabinet of His Majesty. The Senate," *TsGIAL*, folio 1, p. 70.*

12. *Ibid.*, p. 36.

13. *Ibid.*, 341/501, folio 384, pp. 4 and 16.

14. The statue of Peter the Great was erected by Catherine II and is the work of the French sculptor Falconet. On the granite base one finds the simple inscription (in Latin): "To Peter the First, from Catherine II." The enormous granite block forming the base was found at Ljachta, about eight miles from the city, and was dragged with great labor to its present location. According to a popular story, Peter used to climb upon this very rock and gaze at the surrounding landscape while his "paradise" was rising from the marshes. It is called "Thunder Stone" for it is believed that it was once struck by lightning and split in two. Its weight is 166 tons. [P. Steveni, *op. cit.*, p. 241.] Falconet was recommended to Catherine by Diderot. He signed the contract for the creation of the monument on August 27, 1766. In a letter to one of his friends he wrote "I have tried during my work on the model of the statue of Peter I to capture as faithfully as possible the true character of the Russian Emperor, and attempted to express this in a manner which would have been understood by himself. I have decided not to embellish his person with romantic attributes; ancient Russian dress would not have been natural, since he wanted to abolish the traditional Russian dress. The bearskin on which he is sitting is the symbol of the nation which he set out to civilize. Perhaps the Tsar might have asked me, why did I not thrust a sword into his fist? But he made too much use of it during his life, and a sculptor should emphasize only those qualities of character which gave him honor, and cast a veil over those vices and errors which tarnished it." It is therefore not the "Tsar conqueror" that Falconet created, but the "Tsar legislator."

15. *Complete Collection of the Laws of the Russian Empire*, ukase issued April 20, 1738.*

16. "Cabinet of His Majesty," *op. cit.*, *TsGIAL*, 341/501, folio 344, p. 75.*

Chapter 9

1. These dimensions were taken from the so-called Schubert Plan issued by the Military-Topographical depot in 1828.

Key dates in the development of St. Petersburg in the 18th and 19th Centuries*

1703	May 16, St. Petersburg founded. Construction on SS Peter and Paul Fortress and the port begun.
1703	Exchange and Custom houses opened.
1703	Peter I builds himself a house on Petersburg Island.
1703	Founding of Kronschloss Fortress.
1703–1704	City market-place established.
1704	Construction of Admiralty Wharf begun.
1704–1720	Planning and laying out of the Summer Garden. I. Matveev, architect, Ia. Rosen and others landscape architects.
1706–1787	Peter and Paul Fortress built with D. Trezzini as one of the architects employed on this project.
1706	Construction Bureau established.
1710	Alexander Nevski Monastery founded.
1710–1714	Peter I's Summer Palace built in Summer Garden (D. Trezzini, A. Schlüter and others, architects).
1710–1716	Menshikov Palace built (G. M. Fontana and G. Schädel, architects).
1711	Nevski Prospect laid out.
1711	First printing press set up in St. Petersburg.
1711	Construction begun on the dockyard on the Fontanka opposite the Summer Garden.
1711	Construction of Krasnyi and Lebiazhev canals started.
1711–1713	The Arsenal founded. The Galernaia Wharf established.
1711	The Tzar's court transferred from Moscow to St. Petersburg.
1712–1733	Construction of the stone church of Peter and Paul (D. Trezzini, architect).
1713	Botanical Garden established on Aptekarskii Island.
1713	The Senate transferred from Moscow to St. Petersburg.
1714	Krestovski powder-works established.
1714	The Kunstkammer founded.
1714	The first public theater opened in St. Petersburg.
1715	The Naval Academy founded.

* From *Leningrad, Encyclopedical Handbook* (Moscow, Leningrad: The Large Soviet Encyclopedia, 1957).

1715	The Russian School—of belles-lettres—founded.
1717	General Infantry Hospital opened.
1718	Construction started on Ladoga Canal.
1718	Lace manufacture started in St. Petersburg.
1718	Royal tanyards opened in the Vyborg District.
1718	Tobacco manufacturing started in St. Petersburg.
1718–1734	Construction of the Kunstkammer (G. I. Matarnovi, G. Kiaveri, M. G. Zemtsov and others, architects). Now the Museum of Ethnography and Anthropology.
1719	General Naval Hospital opened.
1719	Engineering School founded.
1719	Textile manufacture started in St. Petersburg.
1720	Main City Court established.
1720	Sugar refinery established.
1721	Sestroretski Armament Works established.
1721	Artillery School founded.
1722	First fire brigade organized at the Admiralty.
1722–1742	The Twelve Colleges built (D. Trezzini, architect). Now Lenin State University of Leningrad.
1723	Two Royal Guards Regiments—the Preobrazhenski and Semenovski Regiments—transferred from Moscow to St. Petersburg.
1725	The Academy of Science—created the previous year by Peter I's ukase—opened.
1725	First aqueduct put into service in St. Petersburg.
1725	Granite polishing plant founded in Peterhof.
1727	First bridge across the Neva to Vasilevski Island (Isaac Bridge) erected.
1727–1738	Construction of Admiralty (I. K. Korobov, architect).
1728	The Ladoga Canal opened to navigation.
1731	The Infantry Corps of the Nobility established.
1733	School of Medicine and Surgery opened.
1737	The "St. Petersburg Building Commission" established.
1741–1750	Construction of the Anichkov Palace (M. G. Zemtsov and G. D. Dmitriev, architects; rebuilt by I. E. Starov 1778–1779). Now Palace of Pioneers.
1744	Porcelain manufacture started in St. Petersburg.
1748–1764	Construction of the former Smolny Monastery ensemble (B. F. Rastrelli, architect; rebuilt 1831–1837 by the architect V. P. Stasov).
1752	The Naval Corps of the Nobility established.
1753–1762	Construction of the Nikolski Church (S. I. Chevakinskii, architect).
1754	Loan Bank for the Nobility established.
1754	The Merchant Bank established.
1754–1762	Construction of the Winter Palace (B. F. Rastrelli, architect). Now the State Hermitage.
1757	The Academy of Arts founded in St. Petersburg.
1759	The Pazheski (Cadet) Corps established.
1759	The Tuchkov and Sampsonievski bridges opened to traffic.

1761–1765	Construction of the Nikolaevski Orphanage. Now the Leningrad Pedagogical Institute.
1761–1785	Construction of the Great Gostinyi Dvor (J. B. Vallin de la Mothe, architect).
1762–1796	Period of activity of the Commission for Stone Construction in St. Petersburg and Moscow.
1763–1767	Construction of Dvortsovaia Quay.
1763–1767	Construction of the Hermitage Bridge.
1764	The Pedagogical Institute for Ladies of Noble Birth (Smolny Institute) opened.
1764–1767	Construction of the Small Hermitage (J. B. Vallin de la Mothe, architect).
1764–1780	Construction of the embankments on the left bank of the Neva, now called Kutuzov Quay.
1764–1788	Construction of the Academy of Arts building (A. F. Kokorinov, J. B. Vallin de la Mothe, architects).
1764–1788	Construction of the Angliiskaia Quay (now Red Navy Quay).
1766–1782	Monument of Peter I erected on Senate Square (E. M. Falconet, sculptor).
1768	The St. Petersburg Vaccination Center established.
1768–1785	Construction of the Marble Palace (A. Rinaldi, architect). Now Leningrad branch of the Central Lenin Museum.
1770	First public art exhibition in the Academy of Arts.
1770–1784	The ornamental fence between the Neva embankments and the Summer Garden erected (Iu. M. Feldten and P. E. Egorov, architects).
1770–1790	Construction of the Brantski Palace (later Iusupov Palace). In 1830 completely reconstructed by the architect A. A. Mikhailov. Now used as the regional house for teachers.
1771–1784	Construction of the Old Hermitage (Iu. M. Feldten, architect). Now the State Hermitage.
1774	The City Court established.
1775	The Charity Board established.
1776–1781	Construction of the Kamennoostrovski Palace (Iu. M. Feldten, architect, according to a design by V. I. Bazhenov).
1780–1789	Construction of the Fontanka embankments.
1782	Police Office established.
1782–1789	Construction of the Main Post Office (N. A. Lvov, architect, reconstructed 1803 by the architect E. T. Sokolov, again in 1859 by the architect A. K. Kavos, and finally in 1903 by the architect L. I. Nivikov.
1783	The Russian Academy of Literature founded.
1783	The Central National Institute for the Education of Pedagogues opened.
1783–1787	Construction of the Hermitage Theater (G. Quarenghi, architect).
1783–1784	The Tavricheskii Gardens planned and laid out (V. Guld, landscape architect).
1783–1789	Construction of the Tavricheski Palace (I. E. Starov, architect).

1783–1789	Construction of the main building of the Academy of Science (G. Quarenghi, architect).
1783–1790	Construction of the Assignate Bank (G. Quarenghi, architect). Now the State Economic Institute.
1784	Construction of the building housing the City Duma (council), (G. Quarenghi, architect; the tower was built in 1802 by the architect D. Ferrari; the building was reconstructed in 1840 by the architect N. E. Efimov). Now used as the city station of the October Railroad.
1786	The General Six-Men Town Council established.
1792	The Berda Cast Iron Works established.
1792	The Imperial Glass and Mirror Works established.
1796–1801 1828–1832	Construction of the Public Library (E. T. Sokolov, architect). Now the Saltikov-Shchedrin Public Library.
1796–1803	Construction of the Military Academy of Medicine.
1796–1806	Construction of the new Exchange.
1797–1800	Construction of the Mikhailovski Castle (V. F. Brenna, architect, after a design by V. I. Bazhenov).
1797–1810	Construction of the Moika embankments.
1798	The Academy of Medicine and Surgery opened.
1798–1801	Construction of the Mikhailovski Riding Academy (V. F. Brenna, architect; reconstructed in 1824 by the architect K. I. Rossi). Now the Winter Stadium.
end of 18th cent.	Construction of the House of Iusupov (in the 1820's reconstructed by the architect M. A. Obsiannikov, and again in the 1830's by the architect G. Fossati). Now the K. C. Stanislavski House of Labor.
1801–1811	Construction of Kazan Cathedral (A. N. Voronikhin, architect). Now the Museum of Religion and Atheism.
1801	The Putilovski Works established (on the basis of the transfer of the Imperial Cast Iron Works from Kronstadt). Now called the Kirov Works.
1802	The Philharmonic Society formed.
1803	The Mariinski Hospital founded. Now called the Kuibyshev Hospital.
1803–1835	Construction of the Obvodnyi Canal.
1804	First publication of the *Technological Journal*.
1804–1807	Construction of the Konnogvardeiski Riding Academy (G. Quarenghi, architect).
1804–1810	Construction of the Exchange Building (Thomas de Thomon, architect). Now the Central Military-Naval Museum.
1804–1810	Construction of the granite embankments of the Strelka of Vasilevski Island and the launching ramps to the Neva. (Thomas de Thomon, architect).
1804–1810 1831–1835	Construction of University Quay on Vasilevski Island.
1806–1809	Construction of the Smolny Institute (G. Quarenghi, architect). Now the regional and urban committee of the CPSU.

1806	The rostral columns (on the tip of the Strelka) erected (Thomas de Thomon, architect).
1806–1811	The Gornyi Institute built (A. N. Voronikhin, architect).
1806–1823	The Admiralty reconstructed (A. D. Zakharov, architect).
1811	The Imperial School of Agriculture opened.
1811	The Forestry Institute established.
1812	The cast iron fence around the square near the Kazan Cathedral erected (A. N. Voronikhin, architect).
1814	The Public Library—now Saltykov-Shchedrin Public Library—opened.
1815	The first Russian steamship *Elizabeta* built in St. Petersburg.
1816	The Committee for Construction and Hydraulic Works organized.
1817–1820	Construction of the Pavlovski Regiment barracks (V. P. Stasov, architect). Now the Lenenergo administration building.
1818–1822	The Elagin Palace and Park built on Elagin Island. (K. I. Rossi, architect; I. Busch, landscape architect).
1818–1858	Construction of St. Isaac Cathedral (A. A. Montferrand, architect).
1819	The First Engineering School opened.
1819	The First Pedagogical Institute reorganized into the St. Petersburg University.
1819	The Russian Museum opened.
1819–1825	Construction of the Mikhailovski Palace (K. I. Rossi, architect). Now the Russian State Museum.
1819–1829	Construction of the General Staff Building (K. I. Rossi, architect).
1820	The Semenovski Regiment uprising.
1820	The Artillery School opened.
1824	The Botanical Museum and the Botanical Gardens of the Academy of Science established.
1824	The highest flood in the history of St. Petersburg.
1825	The Mikhailovski Park laid out (K. I. Rossi, architect, A. A. Menelas, associate architect; I. Busch, landscape architect).
1825	Decabrist uprising on Senate Square.
1825	The Alexander Mechanical Works established.
1826	The first publication of *Communications Journal*.
1827–1835	Construction of Troitski-Izmailovski Cathedral (V. P. Stasov, architect).
1828	The Technological Institute opened.
1828–1832	Construction of the Alexander Theater (K. I. Rossi, architect). Now the Leningrad State Academy Theater.
1829	The Pavlovski Cadet Corps Building opened.
1829–1832	Construction of Tuchkov Quay. Now Makarov Quay.
1829–1834	Construction of the Senate and Synod Building (K. I. Rossi, architect). Now the State Historical Archives.
1830	The School of Architecture opened.
1830–1834	Erection of the Alexander Column (A. A. Montferrand, architect).
1831–1833	Construction of the Mikhailovski Theater (A. P. Briullov, architect, façade after a design by K. I. Rossi). Now the Small Leningrad State Opera Theater.

1832	The Civil Engineering School opened.
1832	The Military Academy opened.
1832	The Alexander Theater opened.
1832	Nevski Prospect paved with wood.
1832–1834	Construction of the Neva launching ramps with its Sphinxes (K. A. Ton, architect).
1833	Construction of the paved road between Moscow and St. Petersburg completed.
1834–1839	The Club of the Nobility built (P. P. Giacco, architect; façade designed by K. I. Rossi). Now the Leningrad State Philharmonia.
1835	The Gaslight Company of St. Petersburg established.
1835	The Petropavlovski Hospital opened.
1835	The Pulkovski Observatory established.
1835	The Law School opened.
1836	The Pavlovski Women's Institute opened.
1837	Railroad connection between St. Petersburg and Tsarskoe Selo (now Pushkin) opened.
1839–1841	Construction of the Anichkov Bridge (A. N. Gotman, engineer; railings after a design by the architect A. P. Briullov. The author of the entrance sculptural groups is P. K. Klodt).
1839–1844	Construction of the Mariinski Palace (A. I. Stakenschneider, architect). Now the Executive Committee of the Leningrad Soviet of the Workers Deputies.
1839–1852	Construction of the New Hermitage (L. Klenze, N. E. Efimov, architects). Now the State Hermitage.
1842	Construction of the Konnogvardeiski Boulevard. Now Profsoiuz Boulevard.
1843	Start of construction of the Petersburg-Moscow Railroad.
1847–1852	Construction of the Bolshaia Neva embankments. Now Lieutenant Schmidt Quay.
1848	The Light Neva Steamship Line established.
1849	The Main Observatory established.
1850	The Hospital for Day Scholars founded (Maximilianovskaia Hospital).
1850	Construction completed on Blagoveshchenski (from 1855 Nikolai) Bridge project. Now Lieutenant Schmidt Bridge. Designed by the engineer S. V. Kerbedz.
1861	St. Petersburg University closed after student riots and agitation.
1862	The Nobel Machine Tool Manufacturing Works established.
1862	The St. Petersburg Conservatory founded.
1863	The Obukhovski Steel Foundry established.
1863	Construction of tramway system begins.
1863	Kerosene street lighting introduced.
1863	Water aqueducts introduced in central part of city.
1863	The first Russian Mutual Credit Company established in St. Petersburg.
1869	The St. Petersburg Munitions Works established.
1869	The International Bank of Commerce founded.
1871	The Russian Foreign Trade Bank founded.

1872	The first volume of "Das Kapital" by K. Marx published in St. Petersburg.
1873	Meeting of the City Duma according to the City Statute of 1870.
1873–1874	Construction of Admiralty Quay.
1873	Alexander Park laid out. Now Gorki Park.
1873	The Putilov Works Stock Company formed.
1873	The St. Petersburg Wagon Manufacturing Works established.
1875	Alexander Prospect built into a boulevard (now Dobroliubov Boulevard).
1875	Admiralty Quay planted with trees and greenery.
1875	Aqueduct water supply initiated on Vasilevski Island and in the Petersburg District.
1875–1879	Construction of Liteiny Bridge over the Neva.
1876	Water supply brought to the Vyborg District.
1878	The Erikson Telephone and Electromagnetic Manufacturing Works established.
1879	Electrical lights installed on Dvortsovaia Bridge.
1879	The Rops & Co. Oil Refinery established on Petrovski Island.
1880	The first worker's newspaper *Rabochaia Zaria* published in Russia.
1881	Tsar Alexander II assassinated.
1882	Leather and shoe manufacturing established in St. Petersburg. Now called the Skorokhod Works.
1883–1884	Activity of the first Social-Democratic group in St. Petersburg.
1883	First electrical station in St. Petersburg.
1884	Nevski Prospect illuminated by electric lights.
1887	The Langenzippen Mechanical Pig Iron Works established by Langenzippen & Co. in the Petrograd District.
1887	Construction of a boulevard at Malaia Koniushnaia (Sofia Perovskaia Street).
1892	The Nevski Chemical Works established.
1895–1898	Construction of the Officers Club. (Now the House of Officers.) A. I. Gogen, architect.
1896	The first movie theater opened.
1897	The Women's Medical Institute established.
1898	The Electrotechnical Institute opened.
1898	The Russian Museum opened.
1898	The Aivaz Machine Works established (now Engels Works).
1898–1899	Construction of three central electrical stations, near the Obvodny Canal, the Novgorod Street, and the Fontanka, called the 1st, 2nd, and 3rd LGES.
1898–1900	Construction of the building for the Electrotechnical Institute (A. N. Vekshinskii, architect).

Index

Academy of Arts, 65, 133 ff., 142, 159, 199

Academy of Sciences, 19, 46, 65 f., 72

Admiralty, 7 ff.; axis of, 120 ff., 170, 175, 178, 185 ff., 196, 199; description of, 7 ff., 37 f.; development of 77, 79, 210; façades, 128–30, 149, 169, 174–76; as focal element, 28, 35–37; as fortress, 8, 28, 120–23, 125 ff., 129, 176; new, 31 f., 91; old, 13, 47, 77 ff., 90, 106 f., 108, 210 f.; reconstruction of, 77 ff., 80, 103, 105–31, 183; relationship to surrounding spaces, 146, 149, 158, 164, 168 ff., 172, 174, 183–85, 187, 191, 193, 209; as ship building wharf, 8, 28, 210; sidewings, 112 f., 117–19, 124 ff., 127, 168–70, 172 f., 174 ff., 178; site selection, 7 ff.; size, 135; tower, 36 f., 47, 77, 86, 90 f., 108 ff., 111–14, 119 ff., 182, 189, 201 ff., 204, 206–9; transfer to St. Petersburg, 7

Admiralty Boulevard, 121 f., 126–28, 149 ff., 153, 158 ff., 176–78, 183 f., 186, 193

Admiralty District, 6, 8, 13, 17, 35, 74 f.; development of, 27, 29, 30 ff., 46, 48–50, 53, 64 f., 76 f., 78 ff.; position of, 63 f., 77, 79, 87, 106, 197, 203; relationship to surrounding spaces, 197, 203; plan-

ning of, 37 f., 46 ff., 76, 209; removal of wood structures from, 30

Admiralty Island, *see* Admiralty District

Admiralty Square, 76, 83, 121–28, 147, 149 ff., 155, 159, 176, 178 ff., 183–87, 193

Admiralty Tower, *see* Admiralty

"Age of Empresses," xxvii f.

"Age of Tsars," xxvii ff.

Alexander, Grand Duke (Alexander Nevski), xvi

Alexander I, Tsar (1801–25), xxvii, 86, 100 ff., 106, 118 ff., 122 f., 162 f.

Alexander II, Tsar (1855–81), xxviii f.

Alexander III, Tsar (1881–94), xxviii

Alexander Column, 146–54, 183, 188 ff.

Alexander Nevski Monastery, 33

Alexander Theater, 176, 188, 206

Alexis, Peter I's son, xx

Amsterdam, xix, 25 f.

Angliiskaia Quay, 8, 37, 50, 61, 67, 76, 108, 117–19, 168 f., 197–99, 201

Anichkov Palace, 104

Anna, Empress (1730–40), xxvii, 28, 30, 31

Apraksin, Count, 28 f., 31

architectural competitions, 43–45, 133 ff., 156, 162, 166 ff.

architectural features, *see appropriate individual spaces or buildings, e.g.,* Admiralty, Dvortsovaia Square, etc.

Arkhangelsk, xiv

axial, axis, 126 ff., 153, 169–70, 177 ff., 182, 186 ff., 189, 191, 196 ff.; *see also appropriate individual spaces or buildings, e.g.,* Admiralty, Dvortsovaia Square, etc.

Azov, port of, xiv

Baltic Sea, xiv; xvi ff.; 6, 13

Baroque, 113; Rastrelli's, 144, 146; tendencies, 173

Berger, Georg Christopher, architect, 45

Betancourt, Count, 97, 100, 157 f.

Birzhevaia Square, 53

Bolshaia Neva, *see* Neva River

Bolshoi Prospect, 64

Briullov, A. P., architect, 152–54

building commissions, *see* commissions

canals, *see* St. Petersburg

Cape of Vasilevski Island, *see* Strelka

Catherine I, Empress (1725–27), xxvii

Catherine II, the Great (1762–96), xiii ff., xxvii f., 58, 74, 77, 133, 136

central ensemble, *see* St. Petersburg

Classicism, academic, xxvii, 91 f.; ideals of, 146; in 18th century, 40 ff., 59, 61 f., 65, 86, 128, 196; in 19th century, 71, 86, 129, 148 f., 195 ff., 204; of Rossi, 146; Russian, 45, 51, 79, 195 ff.

climate, v, xxii

commissions, 30–34, 42–45, 58, 86, 88 f., 94, 97–102, 123, 132 ff., 157, 159, 179

competitions, *see* architectural competitions

continuous façade, *see* "unified front"

Corinthian Order, 174

cupola, 156; of St. Isaac, 156, 162 ff., 165 f.

Delta of Neva River, *see* Neva River

Doric Order, 91, 170, 174

Dvortsovaia Quay, architectural features of, 50–55, 58–67, 172 f., 210; reconstruction of, 58, 70 f., 76 ff., 85–88, 92 ff., 94, 108, 115, 117 f., 119 ff., 168, 190, 197–201

Dvortsovaia Square, architectural features of, 125 ff., 132 f., 134, 138 ff., 144–46, 148, 152–54, 196; axial composition of, 148–50, 154; description of, 83, 124 f., 132, 135 ff., 138, 147 ff., 154; part of central ensemble, 147 f., 150–52, 174, 178, 183 f., 187–89; planning of, 103 ff., 132–34, 136 f., 140, 148 f.; reconstruction of, 100, 131 ff., 137 f., 147, 152–54, 161, 190; relationship to surrounding spaces, 127, 134, 147, 154, 176, 178, 187; spatial organization, 146–53, 174, 187

Efimov, N., architect, 180 ff., 190 ff.

Elisabeth, Empress (1741–62), xxvii

Ekaterinski Canal, 29, 34, 36 ff., 47, 197, 202 ff., 208

English Quay, *see* Angliiskaia Quay

Eropkin, Peter, architect, 30, 33, 115

Exchange Building, first, 9, 67 f., 70–74, 80, 86, 93, 128; second, 90–94, 128 ff., 196 ff. 199 ff., 210 f.

Falconet, sculptor, 83, 178 f., 195

Feldten, Georg, architect, 54, 56, 60 f., 80, 103, 125, 134 f., 136–42, 144 ff., 154, 196

fires, *see* St. Petersburg

floods, *see* St. Petersburg

Fontanka, 8 f., 31 f., 34, 36 ff., 47, 87 f., 113, 197 f., 202 ff., 207 ff.

fortifications, *see* St. Petersburg

Galernaia Street, 47, 170–72

General Staff Building, 103, 125, 132 ff., 138 f., 140–42, 144 ff., 147–54, 166–68, 183, 187, 192 ff.

Gerbel, architect, 22 ff., 25

Glukhoi Protok, *see* Ekaterinski Canal

Gornyi Institute, 89–91, 128 f., 197–99

Gorodski Island, *see* Petersburg District

Gorokhovaia Street, 31 f., 33 f., 108, 204

Greece, ancient, 2, 91

Greek temples, 91 f.

Griboedov Canal, *see* Glukhoi Protok

gridiron (street layout), 34, 47, 64

Gulf of Finland, xvi, 7, 9, 13 ff., 16 ff., 164, 208

Hanseatic Merchants, xvi

Hermitage, old, 58–60, 134, 154

Hermitage Theater, 58 ff., 61 f., 70, 86

Holmgard, *see* Novgorod

Ivan I, the Terrible (1530–84), xvii

Kazan Cathedral, 91, 103 ff., 188, 204 ff.

Klodt, P., sculptor, 182

Kokorinov, A. F., architect, 45

Korobov, Ivan, architect, 30, 33, 47, 83, 108 ff., 111–14

kremlins, xxv ff.

Kriukov Canal, 29, 37

Kronberg Arsenal, 48 f., 58

Kunstkammer, 9, 65 f.

Kvasov, A. V., architect, 42 ff., 132, 134 f., 136, 138

Ladoga, Lake, xvi, xxii, 7

Landskrona, fortress, xvii

Leblond, Jean Baptiste Alexander, architect, 13–25, 62–64, 78 f.

Leblond's planning project for St. Petersburg, *see* Leblond

Leim, Ivan, architect, 43

Leningrad, *see* St. Petersburg

Lugovaia Street, 30, 103, 134, 135–38

Malaia Neva, *see* Neva River

Marble Palace, 58 f., 61 f., 67

Mariinski Palace, 179 f., 190, 192

masonry construction, xxi, xxvii, 30 f., 42–45

Matarnovi, G. I., architect, 22 ff., 25

Menshikov, Alexander, Prince, xx f., 9, 11, 20 f.

Mikhailov, A. A., architect, 98, 162 f.

Mikhailovski Palace, 100, 104 f., 179 f., 188, 206

Millionnaia Street, 30, 55

Modiui, architect, 98, 159 ff., 162

Moika, 8, 29, 31 f., 34, 36 ff., 47, 103, 111, 147 ff., 150, 179–81, 197 202 ff., 207 ff.

Montferrand, Antoine, architect, 131, 148, 152, 157–65, 177–79, 182

Mothe, de la, Vallin, architect, 45, 59–61, 80, 154, 196

monumentality, *see* scale

Moscow, xix, xxii ff., xxiv, 8, 28, 78

Napoleon Bonaparte, xxviii

Napoleonic Wars, xxviii, 95, 121 ff., 156, 195

Neva River, architectural development of shorelines, 28, 37 f., 46–52, 67, 76–79, 106, 118 ff., 125, 127 ff., 177, 196–99; architectural features, 38, 46–52, 57, 62 ff., 67, 74, 76 f., 78, 169, 174, 189, 201; Bolshaia Neva, 6, 17, 64, 89, 199; bridges, 169, 177, 187, 189, 199; delta of,

31, 37; location of, 37, 40; Petersburg District layout, 46–48, 52; planning of, 31 f., 33, 189; planning concept of, 36; Roman layout of, 34–36; spatial relationship to surrounding spaces, 38 f., 48, 53, 109, 120, 135, 197 f.; system of, 36 ff.; termination of, 36, 47, 128, 189, 209 f.; use as architectural element, 34, 37 f., 79; Versailles, layout of, 34–36

Rastrelli, B. F., architect, 28, 46 ff., 59, 61, 83, 115, 132 ff., 135 ff., 141, 144–46.

Rauch, artist, 176 f.

Razvodnaia Square, 83, 117, 121, 123–25, 159, 179, 183–87, 199–201

regimental quarters, 33 ff.

residential development, xxv, 9, 18, 33 ff.

Riding Academy of the Royal Guards, 83, 125–27, 148–50, 153, 167, 178, 185, 189, 193 f.

Rinaldi, Antonio, architect, 156

Rogervik, port of, xiv

Rome, 34, 36, 91, 195

Rossi, de, Antoine, modelmaker, 102 ff.

Rossi, Carlo di Giovanni, architect, 42, 196; concerning Dvortsovaia Square, 131 ff., 137–142, 148 f., 152–54; concerning General Staff Building, 125 f., 144–46; concerning Nevski Prospect, 204–6; concerning planning of central ensemble, 98, 101–3, 153; concerning Rauch's Columns, 176 ff.; concerning St. Isaac Cathedral, 159, 161 f., 164; concerning St. Isaac Square, 179–81, 190; concerning Senate Square, 166 ff., 169–75, 189

Russia, autocracy, xxviii; capital cities 26; city planning, 25; court life, xxvii ff.; decline in art of city building, xxviii; economic potential in 18th century, 20 f.;

financing of St. Petersburg, xxv; empire, 9; fleet, 114; governmental structure, 94 ff.; heritage, xxiii; history, xvi, 195 f., 209, 211; in 18th century, 20, 25; in 19th century, 80; maritime outlets, xiv f.; militarism, 95 ff., 121 ff., 129 f., 137, 193; political life, 95; provincial capitals, 43; transformation into modern state, xiv; revolution, xxvii f.; traditional city building, xix f., xxv; war with Napoleon, xxviii, 80; war with Sweden, xvi ff., xvii, 6 f., 13 f., 195

St. Isaac Cathedral, 76 ff., 156 f., 193; axial composition of, 127, 158, 169, 178, 182, 189; design of, 159–66; reconstruction of, 131, 151, 156–63, 177, 179, 211; relationship to surrounding spaces, 103, 166, 169, 179 ff., 185, 187, 190, 193, 201 ff.

St. Isaac Square, 83, 104, 156, 181; as part of central ensemble, 187 ff., 190 ff., 192, 202 ff., 208 f.; description of, 179; reconstruction of, 179–81; relationship to surrounding spaces, 185, 203, 208 ff.

St. Peter's, Rome, 158

St. Petersburg, bridges, 18, 30, 169, 177, 187, 189, 199; canals, xix ff., xxi, 16 f., 18 f., 20, 23 f.; capital of Russia, xxiv f., xxvii, 8 ff., 13, 17, 26; communications, xxviii; compared to Moscow, xxiii; compared to other cities, 200; decline of, xxviii; early years, xxi f., xxiii ff., 27, 40, 210; European influence, xxv ff.; exercise of absolute royal power, xxiv; financing of, xxv; fires, 29 ff., 65; floods, xxi, xxiii, 20, 27; fortifications of, 6 f., 8 ff., 13 f., 15–18; founding of, xiv, xxi f., 4, 13, 78; growth of, xxiv, xxvii, 13, 27; harbor of, 17 ff.; labor conditions, xxi; manufacturing, xxv, xxix, 11; military parades, 47 f., 150 f.; municipal